HOW TO IMPROVE YOUR FINANCIAL LIFE

2021 EDITION

Table of Contents

CHAPTER 1

Why Is Being Successful Necessary?

I must warn you in advance, some of the truths laid out in this book are not going to be what you want to hear or read. ·ey are going to be straight to the point, and feelings will be hurt; I guarantee it. However, I have always been known to be brutally honest, and, in fact, I think it's one of my biggest strengths. A lot more can get accomplished in this world if more people would be honest. Ripping off the Band-Aid, in my opinion, is always better than pulling out the hairs slowly. So I hope you are ready for the truth to set you free!

Some may ask, "Why is being successful even important? Why is it necessary to be successful?"

I would break it down into the aspect of—What makes a human being get out of bed in the morning? What makes a human being tick? Is it the intent to get up and wander around all day long, looking for food and distractions, wondering what's next with regard to a diversionary tactic or something to make us pass the time without having to worry too much about being eaten? Obviously, this is at a base level of existence.

So, if that is what life is supposed to be, then why are we programmed differently? If all we are supposed to be is survivors like the rest of the animal kingdom, then why did the universe, God, or whatever you believe in, decide to make us have an inner voice that tells us we must move forward, we must be better, we must get better every day?

As I have continued to break down success, and human existence in general, I have developed a theory that I call "·e Five Levels of the Achievement Pyramid." If you look at human existence on a basis of purpose, there are five levels on which you can exist or live.

1. Dependency Level: We all come into this world naked, afraid, and weak, with no knowledge, skills, or abilities, and our first level of existence is complete dependency. Obviously, as babies, if we didn't have someone to take care of us and feed us, clothe us, shelter us, and protect us, we would have died very, very quickly. A baby in the wild would obviously perish within a matter of hours.

   At this level, you rely completely on someone else for all your needs. Now, some people only need this for the first eighteen years of their existence, some need it longer, and some people never stop being dependent. Some people, unfortunately, and as sad as it is, are dependent their entire lives. · ey need someone to feed them, clothe them, protect them, and shelter them, and that is really the lowest level of existence. Unfortunately, there are many, many, many people who do not grow beyond this level. I'm sure you even know some.

2. Survival Level: At this level, you grow beyond the dependency level, either because you choose to or because you are forced to. Obviously, if someone is not going to protect and feed you and clothe you, you are obviously going to have to do it for yourself. · is level of existence is usually contrite with severe depression and unfulfillment, with zero goals or true self-worth. In this level of existence, you are simply waking up in the morning, not being happy about it, not being driven, and simply going out in the world with nothing to look forward to and doing the bare minimum that is required to survive.

   What is the bare minimum to feed, clothe, and house yourself? Usually, living paycheck-to-paycheck on remedial jobs—minimum wage or slightly above—with no hopes, dreams, or goals. Again, this is only an existence and is usually marked with heavy depression, lack of self-worth, mental illness, and drug addiction. According to the Center on Addiction, there are nearly forty million people in the United States alone that have a "substance-abuse problem," which is higher than heart conditions, diabetes, and cancer combined! · e Willingway Foundation reports that the highest level of increase in heroin use occurs in Americans with an income of between $20,000 and $49,000. Also, according to America's Health Rankings, suicides are up a staggering 25 percent in the last twenty years! With the US National Library of Medicine reporting that the highest ratios of suicide were, in fact, among the lowest income levels. · is confirms that a lot of these issues will happen in this level of existence because there is nothing else to drive you and nothing else to look forward to. · ese sad realities must be addressed, and the causation must be known! One of the major reasons why I am writing this book is to help people get beyond the Survival Level and out of drug use and suicide. We have to stop pretending as if we don't know the cause. It is socioeconomics, plain and simple. We can change that, and I will fight to do so!

3. Comfort Level: · is level is better known as the middle class, especially in the United States and other first-world countries. According to the US Census data, roughly 30 percent of the American population does rise to this level. · is level is usually marked by people with education, degrees, and skills. Typically, here you will see tradesmen, craftsmen, and creative people. · ey will rise to a comfortable income level where they do not have to live paycheck-to-paycheck, typically making between $60,000 and $100,000 USD per year, which is enough to pay the bills and have a few months' worth of savings, in case there is an emergency. · ey are able to afford a comfortable home, usually something in a middle-class neighborhood, and own a nice car. · ey have decent credit. · ey can go

out to eat. · ey can go on vacations once or twice a year. · is is a very, very comfortable level of existence, a very comfortable level of achievement.

Depression, alcoholism, and drug addiction are still prevalent, but it is less widespread than at the Survival Level. Interestingly, according to the Australian Journal of Public Health, alcohol abuse actually increases in the middle class. While no known reason exists, I surmise that it is due to increased availability as well as overall general boredom and the need for an escape. Typically, depression and unfulfillment are still rampant at this level due to the fact that there is zero growth. Once many people get to the Comfort Level on the Pyramid, there just is no further achievement, which means you will fall into depression. You will fall into the inability to be truly self-fulfilled. For many, growth stops, and you just simply wake up each morning, get on the hamster wheel, and start pedaling.

Again, this is nothing I would recommend. Most people do fall into this level and below, and it is unfortunate that they do not grow beyond them.

· rough this book I want to make sure you have the tools to go beyond this level because only beyond this level is there a true self-fulfillment, true happiness, and true purpose. Alcoholism, drug addiction, and depression are far less prevalent disappear beyond this level.

· e next two levels are the levels that you need to strive for.

4. Prosperity Level: · is is what I try to coach everybody to do. · is is where I say, "Look, this really has to be your minimum achievement level." · ere is a level above this, but this is the one that really puts it all together. You will have a happy, satisfied, and goal-oriented life at this level. You will feel self-fulfilled. You will be able to help your family and many people. You will be able to have true financial freedom.

· e Prosperity Level is reserved for people who have a higher income level, with incomes from $100,000–$500,000USD per year. At this level, you have successful business owners and professionals like doctors, lawyers, high-level salespeople, and other licensed professionals. · is level is not easy to get to. · ere is a reason why this level is the gold standard of most societies of achievement. As a matter of fact, probably less than 5 percent of the people in even in the United States ever reach the Prosperity Level, and worldwide, you probably have less than 0.1 percent to ever reach this kind of level.

· at said, it is absolutely achievable for anyone. It is something you could absolutely aspire to as an individual. You can even do it without a college degree! You just need to have some tools, some knowledge, a mentor, a plan, and you have to take massive action. So, this is where I want to take each and every one of you reading this book. · is is the level that I want every single person who reads, hears, or finds these words from somewhere to take. Wherever you are, I want you on the Prosperity Level!

I'm sure you're asking yourself, how do you get there? Well, it isn't easy that's for sure, but it is simple. · at is good news, right? Simple! However, before you think I'm selling snake oil let me be brutally honest! · ere is a very specific list of ingredients that is required to reach this level and none of them are easy. · e main ingredients are two things: hard work and skill set. As easy as or as simple as it sounds, there are some major moving parts to it. First, you need to have a tremendous work ethic, which we will get on to in the subsequent chapters of the book. But, right now, I want you to focus on the fact that this is very achievable by most! However, let's be honest it is the Prosperity Level and if it were easy more people would live here. It is where you will make a tremendous amount of income. You will save. You will invest. You will pay off your debts and be debt-free. You will have true financial freedom, no longer working paycheck-to-paycheck. You will have a purpose. You will wake up each morning with the feeling that there are goals to achieve, things to get done, and milestones to hit. · ere will be no angst of depression, because you will live a goal-oriented life. · is is really where true happiness and self-fulfillment kicks in, and you can become a truly self-fulfilled person with a true purpose in life.

· is level is pretty amazing, and I don't begrudge anyone on the Prosperity Level. I have been on it for twenty years now. It is a fantastic level. And, again, every day, I wake up with purpose and gratitude in my heart. I have clarity. I have never been depressed in the last twenty years, not for a single day, no matter what challenges life serves me, because I stay focused on goals, achievements, and getting better and moving forward every day. · e power of that cannot be understated. · is is what you MUST achieve! · is is where I hope everyone makes it.

· at said, yes, as amazing at is sounds there still is a fifth level.

5. Legacy Level: · e fifth level of the achievement period is something I call the "Legacy Level". Now, few people—very, very few people—ever achieve the Legacy Level of achievement. On this level, we are talking not really about income anymore. It is more about impressive net worth, ability to influence, capability, resources, and things like that. We are talking about large businesses and fortunes that will be left to children and grandchildren. We are talking about the ability to become a true giver where you are able to help people on a daily basis, whether financially, philosophically or motivationally. You are able to be a mentor to people, a true leader. You are able to really help your community and even your world on a mass scale!

True legacy means something that will live beyond you. When you pass on to the next realm, you can leave something of significance for others and for your family. · ere is a history of you helping people beyond just your immediate family. · at is true legacy. · at is what we should all aspire to. And that is where I wish to help us all ascend. And that is really where true self-fulfillment—a state of Zen, if you will—is achieved, knowing the legacy you are going to leave behind makes passing on to the next realm that much easier.

· e Legacy Level is what I am now striving for. And I hope this book has something to do with my personal achievement in doing so. I can only be successful if I help with your achievement of higher levels in your own life. For me, this book is going to be a huge part of my legacy. I want to create a legacy where I help as many people as I can. I have been prosperous for a long time. I am financially independent. I own several businesses, all of which are very successful. I can come and go as I please. I can help many many people and do.

However, I want to help thousands, even tens of thousands, and hopefully even millions, of people to achieve their goals and freedom the way I have. · at is why I am writing this book. It is also why I am committed to ascending to the final level, which is the Legacy Level. I have all of the material wealth anyone deserves. Now I want to create something that will live beyond me and be passed down long after my death. Something I can truly "take with me" to the grave.

So then, now that we understand the Achievement Pyramid and the different levels, I am sure the next question you will ask me is, "· is seems like a lot of work. "Why" would I want to do all this work? "Why" would I want to make all the sacrifices these levels clearly are going to take? Right? Trust me you absolutely do and let me explain.

· ere are many reasons, and they are all excellent reasons. However, the first and foremost is your own "why" not mine. · ere is also the "who" you must consider, but even before the who comes the why. · e why is, "why" should you do it? Well, I touched upon it a little, obviously, in describing the Achievement Pyramid. · e why is kind of built-in. · e why is a life of happiness and self-fulfillment, a life that is not contrite with depression, anxiety, and lack of self-fulfillment, where you may be exposed and subject to drug addiction, alcoholism, and domestic violence, where you are just an angry, unhappy person. · at is the "why".

Human beings are put on this planet to be prosperous. Anyone who believes in God—and I certainly do—knows the Lord wants us to prosper in all we do. Well, that prosperity is what we are built for. Prosperity is in our DNA. We have to be prosperous. If we are not, we will not be happy. · at is the deal. I didn't make these rules; I just understand, and I follow them, and in following the rules they have never let me down, not one time. If you are not looking to grow as a human being, then you are going backward, and you will be depressed. You will not be happy. Without achievement happiness is simply not possible.

· ere is one very important thing you must understand about happiness. Happiness does not come from the outside in. Happiness comes from the inside out! Now, I want you to take a moment and think about that. What does that mean? Well, a lot of people run around trying to be happy. I'll buy a new car; maybe it'll make me happy. I'll buy a new house; maybe it'll make me happy. I'll get a new boyfriend, a girlfriend. I'll get married, I'll have kids; maybe it'll make me happy. I'll go to a nice dinner to try to be happy. I'll go to a movie to try to be happy. I'll go on a vacation; that'll make me happy, right? Wrong! All of them, while they have their own benefits—and, certainly, a human loving you or getting love in return is one of the greatest gifts we can have—don't confuse a gift of any kind with true happiness. Love and happiness are two very different things.

True happiness can only come from inside you. It is only achieved, in my opinion and experience, by being self-fulfilled in what you are producing for the world, meaning we will only gather happiness for ourselves by the measure of what we do for others, and it is in a direct proportion to what we do for others that happiness can occur. · e amount of happiness you will feel and achieve by helping one other person is then doubled by helping two, three, four, ten, fifty, hundred, thousand, and so on. · e more people you can help and to the greater degree you can help them, the happier you will be. If I help one person mow their lawn, I can feel good about that. I can feel happiness. I have helped someone. I have solved a problem for them. I can feel a certain level of happiness. Now, every problem I solve for someone that is larger than mowing their grass, or cleaning their house, or taking their laundry to the Laundromat will make me happier. Understand the level of problem I solve directly affects my amount of happiness.

⋅ erefore, there are two things that are going to go into your happiness: the number of people you help and the size of the problem you help them with. ⋅ e bigger the problem you solve for the people you help, the happier you will be. Understand that. ⋅ at is liberating. Once you understand how happiness works, at its essence, and understand that it comes from within, not from without, then and only then will you unlock your ability to be happy. ⋅ ere is nothing you can go do besides helping others that is going to bring you happiness. Happiness is you helping others, plain and simple. ⋅ at is the "why" and it's a must.

⋅ e "who" is also very important and the who is at first your immediate circle. You always want to start with those people. Now, we are going with the who in your life. You want to start with your immediate circle, obviously: your spouse, your boyfriend, your girlfriend, your children, your parents, your brothers, your sisters, your immediate family. ⋅ at has to be the first "who" in your life from whom you want to move up the Achievement Pyramid for. You want to be able to do as much for your loved ones and your immediate family as you possibly can. ⋅ e more you can do for them, the happier and more self-fulfilled you are going to be. So, your who starts with your immediate family.

Of course, as you climb up the Achievement Pyramid and you get to the Prosperity Level and above, your "who" now has to go beyond just your immediate family. You can be at the comfort level with your family, comfortably earning an income, comfortably having a home, comfortably having a car, comfortably having the money to go to the movies and go out to eat etc. ⋅ at is the Comfort Level. But, regrettably, the problem with staying at this level is that you can never help anyone beyond your immediate circle, and most people even in this Comfort Level, especially the lower end of it, can't even help most of their family. All they can help is their children, maybe an elderly parent or close friend, but they cannot help anyone else. ·ey cannot help their brothers and sisters. ·ey cannot help both their parents. ·ey cannot help their children with bigger problems. Maybe they can afford to put their child through a lower-level state college or something along those lines but Harvard forget about it. Maybe they can buy their child a car, a ten-year-old Nissan Altima for example.

· at, obviously, is where your Comfort Level is going to take you. And, again, it is regrettable, since we would all like to help more than that right? We know we would. Most people at the comfort level go to bed at night saying to themselves, "I wish I could help people beyond just my children, beyond my one parent, beyond getting my kid a ten-year-old car." Of course they would like to help more people. So that is the "who" you are going to pursue next, right? ·e who after your immediate family is your extended family, then it is friends, and then people in general. · e more who's you help, the higher up you will go, the more money you will make, and the happier you will be. · at is why you want to go to the Prosperity Level. So, the "who's" you truly want to help have to expand as you climb the Pyramid.

On the Legacy Level, obviously, the "who's" expand to everyone you can find. · at is my who's, right now. I want to help everyone I can find. And I will go to the highest mountain, and I will yell these words that are contained in this book until every person can hear me. And, if I'm successful, and I know I will be, I will help thousands, perhaps tens of thousands, perhaps even millions of people, climb this same Achievement Pyramid, and I'll directly help expand their "why", and expand their happiness, and expand their "who's". And I will hope, and I pray that each and every one of you can make it to at least to the Prosperity Level. And even join me if you so desire on the Legacy Level. Now that we have the basis for the understanding the Achievement Pyramid and its direct connection to happiness, the rest of this book will show you the way. I blazed the trail. I have paid the price. I have learned the lessons. And now I will share my knowledge and help each one of you climb the Pyramid. So grab my hand and let's go!

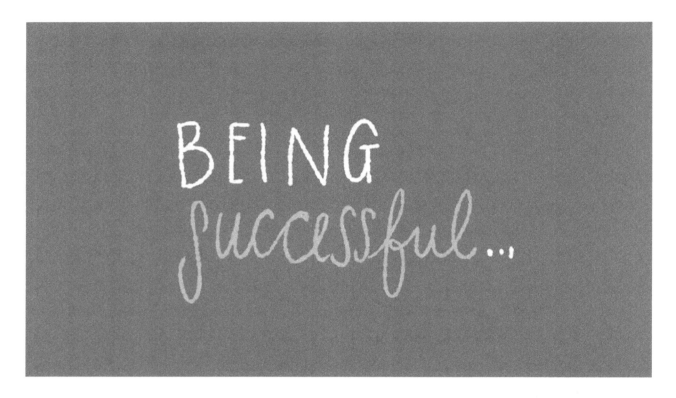

CHAPTER 2

The Reasons Why Most People Don't Make Great Money

·ere are seven big mistakes that contribute to the reason that people don't make great money. ·ere are many reasons that are clearly obvious to most people surely, but the reality of it is that most people fail to make big money because they don't recognize and hence follow certain predictable paths that are not as obvious. Instead they follow paths that seem justified to them, and in doing so create a pattern of not being able to achieve the results that would make them most productive and impactful to somebody who will ultimately control their income—such as an employer or a customer they may be working for—who would be able to compensate them at a higher level.

So, that said, given the different paths there are seven big mistakes we need to identify and control. Of course, there are a lot of mistakes beyond the seven that one can make, but there are seven big ones that really stand out and cover the vast majority of the reasons why people don't make great money and are not quite as obvious to most.

Without going in any particular order, I will start with what I believe to be one of the biggest mistakes, which I call the Delusional Outcome Syndrome, or (DOS). DOS is the false belief that something you are doing is going to have a different, significantly more positive, outcome than what is plausible. Let me give you an example of this. Let us say I'm supposed to walk one mile, and my allotted time to travel that one mile is exactly five minutes. Now, if I'm walking only a mile an hour along this journey, I would be very delusional to think that I'm going to be able to travel this mile in five minutes.

While I may have every intention to walk the mile in five minutes, I have not stopped to calculate my speed in comparison to the distance I have to travel. · erefore, I have a delusion as to what is going to happen after five minutes of me walking at a mile an hour. I will not travel the mile, no matter how much I want to, no matter how much I hope to, no matter how much I believe that will be the result. It is not going to happen. It is a delusional outcome. · at is obviously oversimplified, and I do that to make sure that we understand how this works. Now, of course, we get into a much more complicated situation where we are talking about people who show up to work every day at eight in the morning, and they begin their tasks, and they work from eight to five, mindlessly going through tasks.

· ese people expect the same delusional outcome. · ey believe that working from eight to five, going through some mundane tasks in that time period, is going to ensure they make a lot of money, get promoted, get raises, get bonuses, get appreciation, and eventually get rich; they are going to get all the things that we endeavor for when we take on employment, or a business, if we are a business owner. Obviously, this is a delusion. It cannot happen that way. · e problem is there is no results-driven mentality. No calculation of my speed of travel.

So, what is the counter for the DOS, and how can one switch to results-driven production instead of time-based production? · ink of it this way, instead of simply waiting to watch the span of the day pass, hoping there are results in the direction you want, realize that it does not matter how much time it takes; the outcome is what matters. If you are results driven, you never run the risk of DOS. If I know I have five minutes to get one mile, I will simply calculate how fast I must travel. · en, I will simply start moving at the needed rate of speed, and, sure enough, in five minutes, I will have arrived at my destination of exactly one mile. With any task or goal the calculation can be done the same. ·e mathematical methodology remains the same. And so it works, and it works well and becomes predictable.

·e second reason why people don't end up making great money is the Quick and Easy Fantasy, or the (QEF). ·e QEF is a scenario where someone believes that success or achievement can be done quickly and easily. And while certainly certain tasks can be done quickly and easily, there is no such thing as a quick and easy way of gaining a truly valuable skill set. Applying time to the skill set yields production, production equals value, and value equals remuneration.

·e QEF is something many many people have, and they usually don't end up ever making great money. ·ey simply believe that there is a way to do something quickly and easily instead of understanding that they must do the things correctly and in a fashion that will result in the desired outcome.

·ere is no such thing as quick, and there is no such thing as easy when it comes to obtaining skills, and there is certainly no such thing as quick and easy. Producing significant income or revenue must be a skill that is driven for a certain outcome that has a value that will then equal the pay that I receive in exchange for that agreed-upon value. I must focus not on whether it is quick or easy; I must focus on the outcome, to achieve the value that will then earn me my money. Stop thinking that things can be quick and easy. ·ey cannot or at least that should never be the focus. Instead, be results driven and then your productivity and income can be predictably controlled and incrementally increased over time.

·e third big mistake I see people making is having a negative mentality. ·is negative mentality can be across the board but it typically is found most prevalent in a work environment; it is with the boss, customers, and coworkers. ·is can also happen if you are a business owner. You can have negativity with your customers, your partners, your employees, outside forces and so forth.

·e problem with a negative mentality is that it traps you into a situation where you cannot think clearly. You do not move with purpose, and therefore, you are not driven toward outcomes. Instead, you are driven by tasks, and, unfortunately, if you are being driven by tasks, it will result in the first mistake, which is the DOS. If I have a negative mentality, I will allow myself to be task driven, and the next thing you know, I will then allow myself to expect a delusional outcome, and I will fall back into mistake number one. · is is a vicious cycle indeed and it is far too common.

What is the cure for this? As cliché as it is "· e glass is always half full" approach is the cure! Of course there are always bad things that will happen. · ere will always be things that will offset your day, week, or even month; however, you cannot have a negative mentality toward it. You certainly cannot have a negative mentality toward your boss, customers, partners or coworkers. Despite how you may feel, you must control your emotions in the face of the negativity, and you must turn it back into a positive. You must think positively about your boss, customers, partners and coworkers. Let's call them all "Money Partners" so you can begin to understand **why** you must think positively of them at all times.

· ere is a very simple trick that I use to achieve this positivity, which is simply to say "· ere's something good this person who is being difficult is still offering me". For the boss, you say I'm going to look forward to a paycheck, a raise, or a promotion. · ink of your boss in those terms, and it will change your mentality from negative to positive, and you will be able to move quicker and better and the same would be said regarding co-workers and partners. With customers—whether you are an employee, a manager, or an owner of the company, customers, while not always right, unfortunately, will always control the value of your work, and thus the pay. · erefore, you must always be aware of the fact that the customer drives the value, which then drives the pay that you are going to receive. A customer who is not happy will be a low-paying customer. A customer who is happy will pay more and pay quicker. · at is a fact. · erefore, never approach your customers negatively. Always approach them with a positive mind-set, despite the challenges you may face. Customers can be irritating and can get on our last nerves, but we must always keep in mind that customers are the ones who pay the bills and thus decide the pay we will receive for the value we provide.

So, when you want to be paid more, which is the purpose of this book, you must have a happy boss, partner, co-worker or customer. How do you do it? Simple. You solve their problems, and you seem empathetic to their situation and feelings. Whether you agree with their complaint or not, still fulfill it, and make them feel that you are on their side. "I understand how you feel. I completely get where you are coming from. Let me find a solution." · ose are the things you need to say to your money partners. You cannot berate money partners or tell them they are wrong. · ey will then be unhappy, and they will then not want to pay or contribute more.

Again, they are not always right, but they control the outcome of the pay you will receive. · erefore, you must always make them satisfied and fulfilled. It is a very simple system that I use. You do it with empathy. Try to understand their feelings and their concerns, and simply tell them you will find a solution. · e fact that you care, in and of itself, will typically make them happy or compliant to the degree needed to guarantee top pay for your value.

· e third part of this negative mentality is the coworker mentality. Certainly, there are things your coworkers will do that you do not agree with. What you do have to understand is that the coworkers are helping you add value to the results you are producing. · erefore, you must be aware of their happiness too. Similar to a customer, they are going to help decide how much value is going to be provided and, ultimately, what the result will be. Happier coworkers will help you achieve greater production, which will equal to a greater value, and therefore a higher rate of pay. · erefore, happy coworkers help you make money, while angry or unhappy coworkers will cost you money. So, what do you want to do? Do you want to make more money or less money? Make your coworkers happy! How do you do it? Same thing you do with the customers. You don't always have to agree with their thinking as of course they are not always right. But since they do affect your rate of pay, always be empathetic to how they feel that is not the same as agreeing with their view but it is even more powerful.

Being empathetic with somebody is not the same as being sympathetic. Empathy is simply an understanding of how someone would feel. It is not an agreement of their conclusions. I may not agree with what they are thinking or saying. However, I can still understand it, and I can lend them some empathy with regard to those feelings.

· erefore, dealing with a negative mentality at work or in your business is simple. Remember that your money partners don't have your worst interest at heart. · ey don't want what is bad for you. Sure, some money partners are nicer than others, some are more patient than others, and some are meaner than others. It is what it is. Do not let that control you or your work environment. Instead, you control your work environment. · e way to deal with a boss who has a negative mentality is by you having a positive mentality. How do you do it? · ink well about your boss, and understand that they want ultimately what you want, which is a better production, which will increase the value, which will then have the customers pay more. What you need to do is help them produce those goals so that they are happy with you and therefore increase your rate of pay. Again, a negative mentality serves no purpose whatsoever outside of lowering your ability to have the positive impact you need, which will lead to a decrease in value as well as a decrease in production, and therefore a decrease in the rate of pay. Negativity equals a decrease, and positivity equals an increase with everyone, every time, in every situation. Do not forget that.

· e fourth big mistake I see being made is the "Trying to Survive and Not · rive" mentality. In this situation, as a worker or business owner, we are looking to survive and not to thrive. When you show up to work, you ask yourself if you can just make it through the day. I can't tell you how many countless memes, quotes, proverbs, and comments I have seen people make showing up to work on a Monday. "I hope I can just get through the day. I hope I can just make it till quitting time. I hope that I can just hang in there long enough to make sure that I don't get fired or go out of business." · ese are all survival mechanisms, and if you are showing up at your job or at your company, and your intent is to survive, let me tell you, you are in for a world of hurt.

If you want to guarantee that you are going to make less money, then show up to work trying to survive. · at is exactly what you are going to do. You will not be results driven. Instead, you will be task driven, which will lower your production, and thus lower the rate of pay. Not much will get you paid slower than approaching your work in the survival mentality instead of the thriving mentality. Don't do it. It will sabotage what you are trying to do.

So let us talk about how to thrive. How do you thrive? Well, you show up to work not saying, "I hope I survive." You show up to work grateful that you have a place of employment or your own business and for the opportunity, this day has bestowed upon you. You show up and ask, "What can I accomplish today that is going to add tremendous value to the people around me and serve the customers who are coming to this business?" And, again, whether you own the business or whether you are an employee, it does not matter. It is the same thing and hence the same approach.

· e better the business does, the more opportunity there will be for you, and the greater chance you have for increased pay. · e mentality you need to show up to work with is, "I'm here to thrive, NOT here to survive." Choose to own your day. Approach it with this mentality each and every morning, and I guarantee your days will be better and more productive, and they will help you add value and increase the rate of pay. · rive; don't Survive.

· e fifth reason people don't make great money, and this is similar to the survive but not thrive mentality, but not to be confused, it is trying to do the bare Minimum. In this situation, what people do is they just try to do enough not to get fired or not get a customer complaint. · is is typical of the average worker and business in this country. Unfortunately, they will show up to the business with a negative mentality, wearing "Survive, not · rive" T-shirts, and then say, "I want to do the very minimum I can do to not get fired or upset a customer."

If you are just doing the minimum, here's what's going to happen. · e boss or customer is not going to be happy. · erefore, you are going to have an angry boss or customer. We all like those, correct? · e customers are not going to be happy, and having displeased and unhappy customers will lead to a lower rate of pay. Your coworkers are not going to appreciate the fact that you are putting more work on them and you are taking on less work yourself, so, of course, your coworkers are also not going to be happy with you either. · erefore, they are not going to help you produce. In fact, they will do the exact opposite. · ey will make sure your pay gets lowered and your efforts sabotaged.

Whether they tell you directly and you hear these things from everybody all day or not, understand that this is the dynamic at play. When you understand this dynamic and you approach your work in this capacity, you will understand that you cannot set a tone to do the minimum work possible. · at will lead to a negative outcome, and you will fall victim to a very low rate of pay.

· is reminds me of a story I'll share of a friend of a friend who worked for years at a McDonald's. She, unfortunately, would do the bare minimum at work every single day. As such she never got promoted, or a raise, or any recognition. Every single day that she showed up to work, she was trying to survive, not thrive. She had a negative mentality. She was looking for the QEF, and, of course, she had the DOS, thinking something was going to happen that was going to propel her to success when, in fact, she was doing nothing that would help her achieve a higher rate of pay.

So how do you fix this? Again, don't approach work with the minimums; approach work to always do more. What does that mean? It means that you have to go ahead and move forward and show up to do much more work and offer more value than what you were originally planning to do or what was expected by your money partner.

The sixth mistake is people not improving their current skill set and not learning new skills they can use in the work environment to get a better and more valuable outcome. This is hugely typical of people who do not make much money. Let's call this the "Lack of Skill Syndrome" or (LOSS). These "Loss" people simply don't take enough time to understand the importance of developing new skills and learning new abilities. What I normally recommend is to make sure that you are always improving your current skills and massively acquiring new value-add skills. Whatever your work environment, the more you know about your business and its operations and fulfillment, the more value you are going to be able to bring and hence gain greater value and then get an increase in pay.

If you are talking about how this affects your rate of pay, simply understand that having fewer skills and not knowing as much as you should or could about your profession or your job is going to definitely affect productivity and the value you can provide. The more skills you can bring the high value you have and the higher payer you will receive!

The seventh big mistake is the biggest. I'm sure after these six you must be asking yourself how can there even be a larger mistake? Well there is! And it's so obvious that you have been told to do it since you were 5 years old! It's called Goal Setting (GS). Most people simply don't set enough goals or large enough goals, and that unfortunately causes them to not have great production and hence not make great money. When it comes to goal setting, people always think of long term goals, like five-year goals, ten-year goals, twenty-year goals, life goals, and such, but it must be much more basic than that. The problem that most people have in the work environment is they simply don't set short term, smaller and frequent goals. They don't come in with any kind of a daily plan. They have no daily milestones that they are trying to hit. They are not chasing targets. If you don't have clear daily and weekly goals, you are going to wonder through your day and week aimlessly, and, of course, you are going to end up going nowhere. I see this time and time again.

To help you visualize how bad this is let's compare it to getting your car and driving around, hoping that you accidentally arrive at your destination. If you don't have a map that is going to take you to your destination on this drive directly, how could you possibly believe that you could simply get into your car, drive aimlessly, and wind up in your desired destination? It is simply not possible. Yet people will show up to work every single day with no goal-oriented thinking and think that somehow, magically, they are going to end up in the right place at the right time. It is not going to be possible to end up making good money, getting promotions, charging more and getting a higher rate of pay at your job or business if you have no daily and weekly goals. Short term, daily, weekly and monthly goals must be set, and they must be followed and achieved. Simply if you hit your daily, weekly and monthly goals you'll absolutely meet or beat your longer-term goals. Make short term goals and watch your income soar!

· ese are the seven major mistakes of why people don't make great money at work or in their business. Again, these are very avoidable mistakes. You do not need to make these mistakes. · ey are simply a choice or at least a lac of knowledge. · ere is a very easy solutions for each and every one of these mistakes, and I will go over them to even a great extent later in the book, but I wanted you to understand the macro view of the seven biggest mistakes people make that sabotage their ability to make great money. Really think about those seven mistakes, dissect them, ask yourself how many of these mistakes are you are making at your work or business? And then take an honest, hard look at yourself, and if you are making these mistakes, make a firm commitment to yourself that you are going to change these habits, and you are not going to make these mistakes anymore. · at will be a huge key for you to start breaking through toward achieving your success and true potential!

CHAPTER 3

How to Identify Your Purpose

According to a recent Gallup poll, 85 percent of people are not happy with their current job. Wow. ·at is shocking! Eighty-five percent! ·at is a huge number of people who do not like their current job. Let's dig into this! ·e first question we ask is, "Why is this?" Why do they not like their job or chosen business? Well, I have been coaching, training, and managing thousands of businesses and people for over twenty-five years, and I can tell you that this typically boils down to a lack of purpose. ·ey go to work at 8:00 a.m. and stay there throughout the day. ·ey are there to earn a paycheck nothing more. ·ey are there to survive, not to thrive. ·ey are there just to punch a time clock and earn a small paycheck or to keep the business afloat. Typical symptoms are they cannot wait to get home. ·ey want to leave early and rush through traffic so they can get home, sit on the couch, and watch mindless television, eating a bad diet, getting fatter and getting poorer.

Now, look, I do not judge people for having small dreams, but the reality of it is, if you want to make the most of your life, you have to do something more than plow through a job or show up to a business just to start watching the clock and waiting to get home and on the couch. ·e reality is, without the feeling of a purposeful life where you get up in the morning and you say to yourself, "I can't wait to get to work because I have this larger purpose behind it," you are just existing, and existence with a lack of true purpose is miserable. I don't care where you live, how beautiful the scenery is, how beautiful the people are; if you don't have a purpose, you have nothing, and you will suffer both economically and emotionally if you allow it. After all, it is absolutely your choice and up to you on how you choose to approach your life.

If you choose to have small dreams, then it may be a slow death. It may take seventy or eighty years, but you will be dead. Every moment of every day will be one step closer to a grave filled with boredom, sorrow, remorse, and regrets. It's better to have lived for thirty or forty years and truly lived and been purposeful than to have existed for eighty years and have done nothing for anyone or anything very important. · at is a sad life by definition. Some of you reading this might be saying to yourself at this moment, "Wow. · is is me. · is is how I'm living my life." Even if that is true as long as you have another breath to draw don't quit! I have good news and some bad news.

· e bad news is that you have wasted a lot of time messing around living your life like that. · e good news is that it is not too late to fix it. You can get going right now today. You can change everything. You can make the proper adjustments. You just need to do it and stop making excuses! First, you need to learn how to do it. You need to study and reading this book is an excellent first step. You need to take the time, energy and money, in some cases, and you need to get out there and learn the things you don't know and that you can use to thrive. Learn the techniques and skills needed. Learn the mind-set required. Empower yourself with the knowledge of how to move through a day where you create a great purpose for yourself, a lot of value for others, actually get things done, and stop waiting for the clock to show "quitting time."

With purpose you are no longer waiting for the final buzzer to sound at the end of a day so you can get into the rush-hour traffic, weave your way through endless people who are just as angry and as sad as you are because their day meant nothing, all just to get home, get on the couch, eat junk food, and get poorer and fatter. Don't let this be you. I know these words sound brutal. I know this is upsetting because you wanted that to fulfill you, and you don't want to hear the truth. I know I'm mean and these words sting a little. I know I'm unfair. I know it sucks. I know it's terrible, but this is what you need to hear. · is is what we all need to hear. · is is what I needed to hear twenty-five years ago when I was feeling sorry for myself, when I wanted to quit and give up, and was one of the 85 percent who didn't like what they were doing and didn't feel like they were contributing anything worthwhile. I used to be that person, but the day I found my purpose was the start of true freedom and true happiness, and the beginning of a journey that would allow me to move through life with purpose and finally, truly be happy. I learned that my purpose was to add value to the world and to move through my day such that I actually made things better for people all people I came into contact with and to help them achieved more.

So how do you literally find purpose in any job or business? I am going to share this with you now, so that you can have the same empowerment I had twenty-five years ago that has led me away from being broke, uneducated, unhelpful, a burden on others. I used to be somebody who did not contribute anything to the world, or to my neighborhood, city, or country. · at was a sad existence for me and of course I was depressed most days. But we are going to change that for you, right here, right now.

So, what is meant by a purpose? What creates a purpose that you can use to be fulfilled and make great money? Well let's first talk about what it's not! At the end of the day, work is work. It is always going to be work. Despite people's delusions there is no glorious job. · ere is nowhere you can work that is just amazing every single day, with zero challenges, where you make a ton of money, have no responsibility, and everybody loves you. Hey, when you can find that job, business or career, you let me know. I will be the first one to sign up! · e truth is despite some overly dramatic celebrities that claim they just "followed their passion" to success passion does not always equal purpose. To think that all you have to do is follow your passions is ridiculous. Truth is some people just get lucky. And because they don't want to admit the truth that they just got lucky they chalk their success up to something as silly as "I followed my passion". But following most people's passions will simply lead to being broke and frustrated. So please stop thinking that is the solution because it's not for 99% of us, so get out of that fantasy asap. Fact is work is work. Even professional athletes, actors, singers, the ones we idolize and always want to be like, they work twelve to fourteen hours a day. · ey have to work through pain, through suffering, sickness, production schedules, and they are some of the most insecure people on the planet, to begin with, so imagine that scenario.

In the end, it is hard work for them, too. So, instead of falling for the fantasy that there is a "dream" job here's what will ultimately set you free. What you need to do to define your purpose is, first of all, understand what a purpose is. · ere is a purpose—an underlying reason—behind every action you take. For instance, when I get in my car and I drive down the road, I'm not driving for the sake of driving. I'm driving for the purpose of arriving at a destination. Well, think of this. You don't just go to work every day. You go to work every day to achieve an outcome, the desired result of your purpose. · at is the definition of a purpose, and that is the first part of it you need to understand.

Now, the second thing you need to understand is this: Any purpose that has any value at all can only be established by helping others. So, what is your purpose? Easy. What are you best at helping people learn or do? I am best at helping people learn how to make money, and how to understand the mental game so they can overcome this tough world, and not fall into their own self-loathing and unhappy patterns. · at is what I'm best at, so guess what I'm doing right now? I'm teaching you because I want to help you, and I want you to be empowered. · at is my purpose to help and that can be yours as well.

So, a purpose will always be defined as by helping others. Now, I don't care what job or business you have in this world. I don't care if you are a janitor or working the drive-through window at McDonald's. Now those jobs may be the lowest of the lowest, as far as pay grade goes but they still can have great purpose. If that is where you are, guess what? It is still tied to helping people, and you have to make sure that you understand that. No matter the job you are doing, there is someone else out there you are doing it for, meaning you are providing value to someone else. ·e kid taking my order at the drive-through window at McDonald's is helping me. · ey are adding value to my day. I'm hungry. I need food. I want a pleasurable experience when I go to McDonald's. If the person who is taking my order at the McDonald's window understands their purpose, then they are going to have the ability to add value to the job they are doing. For instance they can add value if they are going to smile and welcome me there. · ey are going to fulfill my order with enthusiasm, and they are going to pay attention to the details they are going to add a lot of value and have a greater purpose. Imagine how much better they would be at providing their service if they believe in their purpose and understand it in their mind. Imagine what their manager would think of them when they clearly understand their purpose is to help people. · at manager or customer would smile and say, "· at person gets it, man. · ey have a lot of potential." · at is what you want.

When you are starting out at entry-level positions or starting a new business, you want your boss or your customer to recognize your potential. · e first thing they are going to recognize is whether you understand your purpose and whether you value others, because, ultimately, that is what you are providing, value! · erefore, that is what you have to keep in mind. · at is how purpose in the workplace is defined. Now, how does it apply to you in your current situation? Right, because the name of this book is "Maximize Your Now." Well, it does not matter what job you are doing or to what level your business is at you are helping someone. · ere is a purpose behind your job. So, what you have to ask yourself is, "Who am I helping?" Put a face to it. Put names to it. Put people to it. Put emotions to it. · at is going to help you identify your purpose really, really quickly and then be able to add more value to what you are doing.

So your purpose is simple it's to help people! Now, don't think of your job as just a job or just a business. Instead, think of it as being a purpose of helping others. ·ink about the joy, the good feelings, the value you can add to the people who are affected by the job you are doing. If I'm a janitor and I'm cleaning a bathroom, there is nothing glamorous about that. But if I keep my mind on the fact that someone is going use this bathroom, perhaps a coworker or a customer, and they are going to really appreciate the fact that the bathroom is clean and that someone thought well enough of them to do a great job in cleaning the bathroom then that is going to reflect upon you and your pride, upon the business, and upon them.

Now, if you approach your workday with that mentality you will not be one of the 85 percent who hate their jobs! No. You will be one of the lucky 15 percent who create higher value, self-worth, the sense of actually having contributed, because you know that you directly impacted people in a valuable way. You made them feel good. ·at is what you need to focus on. ·at is true empowerment. When you can empower yourself and your day with that kind of power, can you imagine the doors that that will open? Because, trust me, it is infectious. People around you, your coworkers, your boss, the owner of the company, your customers they will all see and feel it. · ey will recognize it, and more importantly, they will value it, and this will open up worlds of opportunities for you to earn a higher income.

How can this be applied to taking it further than your current job? Let us just say you are at a starting position with a company or you just started a new business and you say, "I want to take this, carry it forward to other opportunities. How do I do that?" Here is how you do it. To find our overall purpose in life, we all must start at part-time, entry-level jobs. For instance, my first entry-level job was as a landscaping laborer at five dollars an hour as the starting pay. It was the middle of the summer in Arizona, 110 degrees, and I had to dig ditches in solid, granite dirt for 10 hours a day at 5 bucks an hour.

Now, sure I could have been miserable. I could have said how unfair it was and everything, but I didn't do that. Instead, I said, "Who am I adding value to?" Somebody lives in this house where I'm doing this job. Someone owns this building. Someone lives here. Someone works here. ·ey are going to recognize my work. ·ey will notice how great a job I did, and it is going to mean something to them. Because of that, I took a tremendous amount of pride in my work. I realized the value it had beyond the five dollars per hour, and I went to work every day with a smile on my face, knowing the value I was bringing and it had nothing to do with five bucks and hour.

No matter what you are doing, that is how you have to approach it. Now, as I have moved forward in my life—I have come a long way from being a landscaper for five bucks and hour. I may have started there but as of now, having run several multimillion-dollar companies and made millions and millions of dollars—I continue to move through my day with the exact same mentality I had as a landscaper. It does not change because I am doing something different or for a higher rate of pay. I must still approach everyday with the exact same purpose and approach.

So, now, let's talk about what do you want to do with your life? How do you want to scale your value and this purpose? Well, it is different for all of us. Not all of us have the same talents and gifts. ·is does not mean we cannot all contribute just as much value and have just as much purpose as someone else.

Here is how you do it. You have to ask yourself, "What am I good at?" ·ere are different things. I mean, there are a lot of things in this world I cannot do, and I could never do. I don't know how to sew. I am not great at math. I am terrible at higher-level math that's for sure. I can add, dollars plus dollars, you better believe that, but I'm not good at Calculus! So therefore I'm not good at engineering. I'm not really all that good at computers either so imagine the number of jobs and professions I am not suited for a lot! So then I must assess what I am good at and I do know I am a good communicator maybe not even great but at least pretty good, and I'm a great teacher because I find a lot of my purpose in teaching, so guess what? I found my ultimate life purpose and it is to communicate and to teach. So, what are you good at? What are you best at? What do you love to do? Find it. If you love doing it, you are going to be good at it of course. I don't care what it is; being a janitor, a maid, a nurse, a doctor, a lawyer, a music producer, a director, a photographer, a wedding planner. You get my point? It does not matter what you pick. Pick something that you are good at, and be really, really good at it. Take a lot of pride in being the best, the very best. Set your sights on the fact that you want to be the best that the world has ever seen doing it. Say to yourself "I'm going to be the best wedding planner the earth has ever seen. Period." · en, go do it. Learn it. Study it. Get educated. Get mentors. Get coaches. Practice. · ink. Do all the things necessary to be the greatest wedding planner of all time, and you will be able to achieve that purpose and then intentionally add a tremendous amount of value to those people you help. Guess what will happen? You'll be able to charge top dollar and make a fantastic living!

So, that is how you find what your purpose can be. Now, to make great money doing it you have to be good at teaching people this, or you have to be really, really good at doing it for people. So, if you want to make money at it, then you say, "Okay, this thing I'm really, really good at; does it have any value to others? Does it solve a major problem for people?" · at is always what value comes down to: the size of the problem and the amount someone is willing to pay to solve that problem. So let us continue with the earlier example. Some people really get frustrated with their weddings. · ey would pay good money to have someone else plan it all out so they can show up stress-free and just have a great time at their wedding. Need proof? Seek out a very popular wedding planner and see how much they charge. When you pick yourself up off the floor you'll understand my point of value. A lot of people would benefit from that service therefore you could now have a valuable service. Now you must also think scale. So it's a big problem and people will pay a lot of money for someone to really bring value but now how many people can you do it for? Well, how many people can do it for in a month? One a week? Two a week? Five a week? How big are the weddings? · e bigger the wedding, the more the planning. · e more the planning, the more the money you can charge because the greater value you can bring. So, then you can think scale. You have to scale this purpose and this ability if you want to maximize your earning potential. It comes down to two things. How big is the problem, and, therefore, how much money can I charge to solve it? And how many people can I do it for? · at's the essence of scale and its how money is earned for each and everyone of us regardless of the type of job or business. How far you scale will lead to how much money you can make at anything.

· e great news is you can scale anything. Let's apply this thinking to a simple example of selling a hamburger. When a hamburger restaurant first starts, they scale the hamburger. Someone's hungry, they come to the new restaurant. · ey come in and buy some food. "Here's a hamburger. Here you go." Another person's hungry. "Here's a hamburger." "Yum!" How much money was made off that one hamburger? Fifty cents? A dollar? Not a lot. But you know what happened? Right when that was done, that person said, "· at was a fabulous hamburger. You really put your all into it. It was delicious and I'll be back." And then that owner said, "You know what? I think I can feed more people with this type of hamburger." · us, begins the scale of the sales of the hamburger.

· is is obviously oversimplified, but you get what I'm saying. Once you find out what you are good at and you really perfect it, you need to scale it. If it is something small that doesn't make much money every time you do it, but you can do it a large number of times, scale it. Or, if it is something like a wedding planner, or a surgeon, or a lawyer, where you have fewer customers, but it is solving a really, really big problem, and they really need some help, you can't scale quite as easily but you can charge a lot. You can first scale by either the size of the problem or by the number of people you help. · en in both of those situations regardless of the size of the problem you scale both to helping more people with either the hamburger or the professional service. If you solve a lot of problems for a lot of people then of course you make a lot of money!

Now, ultimately, where does this lead beyond just making money? Well, if you are good at something, and it truly helps others, and you do it for a lot of people, then you will create a lot of happiness in your customers. · at happiness will then translate to you serving your purpose, which will then make you very happy. You will be very self-fulfilled. So not only can you make great money at it if you can scale it but you will ultimately fulfill your purpose and create a lot of happiness for others and yourself! Ultimately, your life's purpose is not going to be about the money. It is going to be about the journey of helping people. Now, are you going to make good money while you are on the journey? Absolutely, because you are going to provide a lot of value to as many people as you can. You are going to go out of your way to provide value. So, you are going to make a lot of money, because you deserve to and because you are helping people, but it is about the journey, not about the money.

So, if you want to make a lot of money then make it first about the journey. Focus your energy first on the journey, the people, the purpose, not on the money. Don't go to work today to make a thousand dollars. Go to work today to help as many people as you can help, with as big of a problem as you can help them with using your skills. Doing so and charging a fair price is going to lead to you making a lot of money every time. One final thought is this—make this your mantra: Always be a gift, never be a burden.

CHAPTER 4

Learning to Flip the Mental Switch

It is not easy. Obviously, we all have these inner thoughts. We always have these things in our minds that tell us how to feel and how to act. · ere is a little voice in your head that says, "Don't do it. Don't do it very hard. Don't do it very long. Don't do it very well." · e sad reality of the natural human condition is that we are preprogrammed to be suspicious and negative. It is a fact. I'm sure it comes from something along the lines of protecting ourselves 10,000 years ago, when we were super vulnerable to danger and had to hunt and gather our food. If we didn't suspect everything would hurt us and do everything we could to conserve calories then we would have been placed in grave danger from attack or starvation. · is survival instinct to protect ourselves makes us question every thought and every action.

Obviously, being skeptical in those times had its advantages. If the body is sedentary, it helps us conserve calories, and when food is harder to come by, it is a benefit. · erefore, the natural tendency of a human being is to remain idle, to relax, and not work too hard; only work hard enough to gather, to hunt, to sustain and then be suspicious of everything.

I mean, look at the animal kingdom. · is is pretty much the state of most animals. · e only times they are active is when they are either looking for food or procreating. As fun as procreation is, obviously, it is limited for human beings in a time scale. So, the other factor for us is food. Well, fast-forward; to modern times. We no longer have to go hunt or gather our food. It is available at every supermarket and every fast-food restaurant on every corner. · erefore, with the human condition being as it is, we don't have to work for even that anymore and we are relatively safe given correct decisions.

What ends up happening due to our ancient instinct is the mentality to be negative and suspicious. I'm sure we have all experienced it. We come across people on the street, or among friends and family. True, it is always just a jest, but a typical saying is, "Hey, take it easy. Don't work too hard. Don't stress yourself out." · ese sayings, unfortunately for us, have a deeper meaning. You already have a natural tendency to be negative, and now you have people telling you to relax. We are already programmed to take the easy route, and now people in our lives are telling us to take the easy route. See the problem?

What does this do for your mentality? Well, it reinforces the negative actions. So, when someone does say, "Hey, you need to work hard. Hey, don't take it easy. Get up. Get going. Get moving. Work for fifty hours a week. Work for sixty hours a week and stay late. Come in early," all these things run exactly opposite to what are instinct is and what we have been told, what has been reinforced, and what is our natural tendency, which is to be sedentary. Now you can imagine the kickback your mind has to that. Now you hear the complaining. "Oh, I don't want to have to go in early. I don't want to have to stay late. I don't want to have to work more than I have to work. I don't want it to be hard. I don't want it to be difficult. I want it to be easy."

· en, the default becomes to look for the easy way out, the shortcut, right? Let me tell you something about shortcuts. · ey are never the right way to do anything. · e shortcut goes through the scary forest where the wolf, with the big teeth and the scary claws, is waiting for you, and it is going to devour you when you are not paying attention.

· e problem is that this is going to keep happening. Now, of course, we know that if we ever want to be great at anything, make a lot of money, be successful, fulfill our purpose, and help the most amount of people we can help with the biggest problem we can help them with, well, a shortcut will not be the right way. We are going to require the "long cut", by finding the right way to do it, knowing that it requires more work and more sacrifice. It does require showing up early, leaving late, working fifty hours or even sixty hours a week.

How do we get there? How to go from the problem to the solution? How do we flip that mental switch? Well, let us get into that. · e first thing you need to understand is that it needs to go back to your purpose. If I'm getting up early every morning to help people, if that is my mission, my goal, my purpose, and if I'm bringing joy to their lives, which therefore is bringing joy to me and happiness to me, then all I have to do to really flip this mental switch is to remind myself of my purpose. When you say, "Look. I don't feel like it today. I feel stuck. I feel like I'd like to leave early today. I don't want to work today," remember your purpose. Remember why you are doing it and the people you are helping and the happiness you will bring them. · is will help you to flip the mental switch.

Now, here is what I want you to do. · is has to be something that is immediate. It is going to be something that is quick. It cannot be something that you are saying, "Well, next week, I'm going to help somebody. Next week, I'm going to remember my purpose." No. It is got to be right here, right now. · e easiest way to do it is to say, "Look. I have got to find somebody right now, at this moment, whom I can help." Now, there's going to be nothing faster to flip your mentality than immediately stopping the negative mentality and going to help somebody even with a small problem. If I immediately want to go help somebody, how do I do it? Simple, pick up the phone. Make a call. Run outside. Grab somebody. "Hey, I'm going to help you." Call a client. Go to your boss. "Hey, boss. Is there something else I can help you with?" Go to a customer. "Hey, customer, what do you need me to do right now? Give me something, anything. I want to do something for your right now."

· ey would immediately give you a task; you are immediately helping someone and make that connection. Always make the connection that any and every task you are doing, from cleaning a toilet to brain surgery and everything in between, is helping someone. Remind yourself of that. On the way to do a task, walking down the hallway to do the task, remember that this is to help someone. ·is is going to help Frank, Mary, Bob, Billy, Sally. Put a face to your task and your purpose. Put a name and visualize. Visualize the smile on their face that they will have when they get the value that you are adding to them right now. ·at is going to help you flip the mental switch at any time on command.

Remember also to take lots of action, not perfect action. Don't wait. Procrastination is a success killer, and it is looking for you! And it's a serial killer it will keep coming back again and again. Don't let it find you because you took the shortcut through the scary forest, because if it does, it is going to take you out. So, what do you do instead? You are going to take fast action. Don't wait for it to be perfect action just make it fast. People sit there and think, think and overthink. Don't overthink. Act. Act. Act. Act. I'm not asking you to be reckless. Don't get me wrong. Don't confuse it with being reckless. I don't want you being reckless. I don't want you swerving through traffic at a hundred miles an hour just because you can, all right? Don't confuse reckless with purposeful. Be diligent, but be quick. Don't wait. Take fast action, quick intelligent action. Move, move, move.

Get good as you are doing the skills. Don't think, "I have got to be good, and then get going." No! Get going, and keep getting better as you go. Actions will then drive your purpose, which will then drive your mentality. You will flip the switch, be happy, and feel fulfilled. You will feel the feeling that can only come from helping other people. ·is will flip the mental switch all the time. So just remember this: consistent effort over a long period of time, combined with lots of action, not perfect action, but—let us call it—learning action. Yeah, that is a great term. Learning action is taking action and learning while you are doing it, not waiting to learn it first and then do it. You will never do it because you will never feel ready. You have to start taking action—lots of action—and learn on the fly. Massive Learning Action (MLA) is a big key to success.

Also, you have to make sure that if you get stuck, you just grab something that needs to be done, and you start doing it. Don't wait. Don't procrastinate. · e next lesson in this is to keep in mind that you want to be results driven, not time driven. Imagine you have a customer named Sally. Say to yourself "I have got to help Sally with X. Whatever problem I'm solving for Sally; I have got to get it done. I've got to help her with it. Now, it doesn't matter how long it takes. It doesn't matter if it takes five minutes, fifteen minutes, five hours, fifty hours. I'm helping her with a problem."

Now, what's the problem? Isolate the problem, and now I have got to solve the problem. I have got to fix the problem. I have to give her a solution to the problem. · at is my goal. · at is my drive. Nothing to do with time. How big of a problem is it? · e bigger the problem, the longer it is going to take. I'm not saying you should be slow or inefficient. I'm saying that we should just focus on the result, not the time. You will be surprised how much you can accomplish in a ten-hour workday and how much results you can get, if you move quickly and use massive learning action to guide you.

Nothing is going to flip your mental switch faster than massive action that resulted in a ton of great results for a lot of people who you are helping with a number of big problems. · e amount of satisfaction you will get from that will absolutely fill you with positivity. · at is the secret to flipping the mental switch.

So, what I want you to do right now is put down this book just for a minute, and go do something for somebody. You need to go do it right now. Get it done. Get it done quick. Take massive action. Make it happen. Get your wife a drink. Get your husband a sandwich. Go clean something you have been putting off cleaning. Go grab a screwdriver, and fix the hinges that are loose on the drawers. Just grab it, and go get it done right now. · en, come back, and keep reading and then think about how good that felt. · at, my friend, is flipping the mental switch! Keep doing it all the time until it becomes a habit.

CHAPTER 5

Maximizing Your Current Situation

· e biggest thing I can say about maximizing your current situation is that it must be a multifaceted approach. Obviously, there are many factors that are involved in the possibility of maximizing your current situation, each of which will have an impact, with all of them combining to create a dramatic impact. And, really, the purpose of this chapter is to open your eyes and your mind to the possibility that by tweaking each individual variable, though each one by itself may not make a significant impact in your life on your finances, remember, cumulatively, they certainly will. · e cumulative effect of combining all of the strategies I will provide in this book is oftentimes greater than 50 percent to 100 percent difference in either disposable income and/or debt reduction or a combination thereof, either of which is obviously very significant and for a lot of people, something that can save them years, if not decades, of work-and-lost-income potential. At the end of the day, the truth is you only have so many years to get this done. You can always make more money, but you cannot make more time! Anything you can do to get more done is less time holds the most value.

· ere is a nine-part process that I use that when combined together can make a dramatic increase to your financial life very quickly, the first of which we have already discussed in-depth earlier, which is the quick and easy pay increase. Let's call this the "Magic Nine". Remember our quick pay increase refers to an immediate 10-20 percent increase in your take-home pay, whether it is a job or a business you own. A 10-20 percent pay increase, as you can imagine, is significant, especially if it is applied over a period of months, years, or even decades. · at said, let us move on to the other eight starting with the second way to affect your immediate finances, which is better credit.

Now, better credit obviously has a dramatic impact on your life, on your finances, as you are able to achieve better, cheaper financing. · is can go into not only saving money but also into a dramatic increase in your lifestyle, because the fact of the matter is that a lot of people will pay a significant sum more for the use of credit, be it via car loans or home loans that others.

I will give you a perfect example of what I'm talking about. Let's say your credit score is 580. You go to finance a car. First of all, with a 580 credit score, your chances to get a loan are already going to be very limited. Typically, with that low of a score—anything below 620 or 630—you are going to be limited to about a maximum loan of $10,000–$15,000, if they are willing to lend you anything. · at is going to be the limit of the bank's trust in you, with that low of a credit score. Clearly, with a 580–620 credit score, you have not proven to a bank that you are reliable financially and that you are going to pay them back. · e sad tragedy of it is that I routinely watch people ruin their credit score over very small sums of money. · ey will let some $50, $100, $400 collection account go on their credit report, and that alone crashes their credit score. Or they will run up balances on small balance credit cards that will lower the score to a hundred points in some instances. For example, maybe they have a credit card that has a $500 availability, then they will run it up to $490, the combination of a small collection item for $400, and running up your $500 credit card to the limit is going to be about a hundred-point drop in your credit score. So, where you could have had a 680 and live in a different world using the same amount of money, you now have a 580 and are severely limited over less than a thousand dollars' worth of issues not smart right?

Going back to the car example, what you have to realize is if you are able to finance, let us say a $15,000 car from a subprime car lot, the typical interest rate can be anywhere between 15 percent and 29 percent. If you borrow $15,000 for a car at roughly 25 percent interest, your payment on a 72-month loan would be $400.00—which is equivalent to borrowing $25,000 at a 5 percent rate for the same amount of repayment time. So, the reality of it is that you will end up with the same payment on a $15,000 car due to poor credit than you would otherwise have on a $25,000 vehicle with better credit. If you are going to pay $400 a month for a car, do you want it to be for a $15,000 car, or do you want it to be for a $25,000 car? As you can imagine, a $25,000 car is a significant improvement in your lifestyle over a $15,000 car. Additionally, cars of those levels are able to afford extended warranties, or you are able to buy newer vehicles, which already have a vehicle-existing warranty, thereby that also saves you more money in the cost of repairs over time.

Also, contrary to popular belief, insurance companies typically charge less for newer cars than they do for older cars since the people who drive newer cars are typically more financially responsible. Also the vehicle generally has a better maintenance record and is in a better condition. · e brakes, the steering, the safety features all work better. Typically, since it is newer, it has airbags and other safety features that an older car would not have. · erefore, you also save money on insurance, on the cost of repairs, and you end up with a much more reliable and enjoyable vehicle all at the same monthly payment price. You can imagine the impact that one variable alone can have on your life and your ability to make more money as you have much more appropriate and "reliable" transportation to get you to and from work. We will delve even into greater detail on some of this stuff later in the book so sit tight.

· e third thing you need to consider is obviously any existing bad debt you may have. Bad debt is another situation that you can immediately change, which will have a dramatic impact on your current financial situation. It is imperative to settle up any bad debt immediately so that it does not impact your credit score and also does not detract you from being able to make more money. If you know that you have bad debt and collection agencies and other third parties' attorneys are chasing you for money, it is obviously going to wreck your mentality. ·e mental drain alone is not worth the trouble it would take to simply get it settled up. Don't worry I will get into exactly how to settle bad debt in later chapters.

·e fourth way you can affect your immediate situation and maximize your "now" is understanding exactly how income generation works. We have learned about scale and problem solving so far as it relates to making money so let's dive deeper into income and how it actually works. First, understand that there is no such thing as a passive income. Passive income, in my opinion, is an absolute myth created by people who were intending to sell people a "get rich quick" scheme. Even if you do derive some income from investments, it is not passive. You are actively involved with it, and even if it takes a very limited amount of your time compared to your full active income, it is still not truly passive. You have to deal with, plan for, make arrangements for, pay taxes on, and meet with your accountant about it. You have to manage it, to some extent, and some investment money has to be managed very closely. However, just wrap your brain around the fact that there is no such thing as passive income. It is a myth. It is a mirage, and those who look for it typically perish in the desert. So to be clear there is no passive income. Always remember that all income is active to some degree and as such you must consider the return per hour for your activity in any income stream. ·erefore, don't waste valuable time looking for passive income. Instead just remember to increase the amount per hour you are earning from any source.

·e fifth way that you can dramatically impact your "now" is to understand and control the use of your energy. ·e reality of it is that every day when you wake up in the morning, you have what is equivalent to a gas tank of energy. For Instance a human being only has a certain amount of willpower at their disposal on a daily basis. You have a certain amount of energy you can expand,

and this is especially true of emotional energy. Understand that your emotional-energy tank is a lot smaller than your physical-energy tank, so this is something that you really have to conserve and be aware of; otherwise, you will burn through your emotional fuel early in the day, thereby rendering the rest of your day absolutely worthless. It is imperative that you are aware of how your emotional energy works, and how to conserve it, and it is actually very easy to do. ·e number one hack that I use and teach people on how to conserve emotional energy is to only focus your emotional energy on things that you can actually control. Unfortunately, most people focus a vast majority of their time and their emotional energy on things that are not under their control, worrying about what somebody else is doing or thinking, or a situation that is not under their control. ·ere are certain factors in your life that you just simply cannot control and you need to identify those each and everyday so that you do not waste your emotional energy on them and instead put It to use on things you are fully in control of.

For example, you cannot control politics, the weather, or the mood of the people around you. What you can control is yourself, and therein lies the secret. Only put emotional energy into what you can directly affect. Do not put emotional energy into factors over which you have no control. Doing so will drain your emotional tank, leaving you feeling drained and unmotivated, leaving you to spend the remainder of your day completely ineffective. You want proof of this? Simply log on to your favorite social media platform and watch how many people waste their emotional energy on politics, people they cannot control and other trivial situations. You will quickly see the waste of their powerful emotional energy. So do not fall for the trap of using your emotional energy on these types of things. Instead conserve it and use it where you need it for what your goals and tasks are. You will quickly find you will have more energy and better focus for what really matters and what you can instantly impact.

· e sixth way in maximizing your now is understanding what you can and cannot fix. · is is similar to your emotional energy, and this certainly has a dramatic impact on your emotional energy. But this is a little less philosophical and a little more action driven. · e thing that you want to focus on is that you cannot fix other people. You cannot fix your boss, your coworkers, or your customers. You can persuade them, you can discuss things with them, you can hopefully get fresh ideas and maybe a different perspective, but at the end of the day, you simply cannot fix them. However, you can fix yourself. So, what do you want to spend all your time on? Fixing you. Don't wait for your world to adapt to you. You adapt to the world. · is is a tactic I use in my daily life and it serves me well.

I understand that I cannot control the world. It is what it is. I didn't make the rules or the factors that go into how it all works, but what I can control, and what I'm fully in control of, is how I move through the world and how I respond to it. It is vital that you understand this. Doing so will allow you to take full control of your actions, because you become free of the emotional and psychological chains, thinking that others have something to do with what you are doing. So often, people whom I train wait for someone else to do something so that they can then do something. · at is obviously a big mistake. And when you actually vocalize it, you understand how ridiculous it actually sounds. You are waiting for someone else to do something so that you can take action. What if they never do it? You are going to be stuck in your current situation. · at is simply unacceptable.

So, what you want to do instead is say, "Look, I can't control the world. I can't control the universe. But I can control me." Focus on what you are doing. Get things done, and keep taking action. Keep doing things faster and better. Let the rest of the world adjust to you, not the other way around. · is will have a dramatic impact on what you can get accomplished right here, right now on a daily basis.

The seventh way is to directly control your maximum daily output. Now, what does this mean? Most people, unfortunately, have a very bad habit of wanting to do today's work tomorrow or catching up yesterday's work today. The problem with this is that they are caught in a perpetual loop of never getting today's work done, because they are either catching up yesterday's work or they are waiting and procrastinating, thinking they will do today's work tomorrow. Of course, this is a habitual issue that will create havoc in your life, destroy your finances and your mentality, and make you feel overwhelmed and paralyzed.

This is a key factor. You cannot do yesterday's work today, and you certainly cannot do today's work tomorrow. Maximum daily output simply means that you are going to get today's work done today. You are neither going to think about yesterday's work that did not get done nor about what you are going to do tomorrow. You are only going to focus on what today's tasks are and what today's outcome needs to be. If you stay focused on what is needed for today's outcome, you will spend less energy worrying about another day's production and focus more on today's production. Obviously, today's production will be higher, and therefore, you have now increased your output and your effectiveness. Now, the trick is simply to do this every single day. As long as you do today's work today and get today's result today, you will never feel overwhelmed.

The eighth way that you can immediately impact your now is what I call the "1 Percent Rule." The One Percent Rule is the idea of getting one-percent better every single day. So, today, I am going to be one percent better than I was yesterday. It may not be a huge improvement from one day to the next, but it is an improvement. I will do one percent more work. I will get one percent better skills. I will do something better today than I did yesterday. It is the "one percent rule", and the dramatic thing about it is that is has an incredible compounding effect. While one percent doesn't seem like it is going to be very significant, simply do the math. A one percent improvement every day would have you improve by 100 percent within seventy days, as you are "compounding" the results. Therefore, you would be twice as skilled and twice as effective within three months or less at anything you want to learn than you are today. Within a year, you will be four hundred or more percent better than you are now! Bam imagine what that would do for your income? Get a little better at something every single day. Hold yourself accountable for this simple rule and watch how fast you can improve at anything.

The last and ninth way of the magic nine is really a way of thinking. It's a thought process based on a saying I have heard over and over again through the years. It is an old school saying and trust me there is a lot about the old school that we need to remember. Simply said. "Work hard enough to get your boss promoted." Now think about that. If you are working so hard that your boss looks good, now imagine the impact it is going to have on you, especially if you want to get your boss's job. Get your boss promoted from their current position and guess what their position is now available to you. That is a great way to create vertical movement in an otherwise promotion limited work structure. You may not always have a lot of unlimited upward mobility in the organization you work for, but if you can move those ahead of you up the ladder, it opens up the door for you to also move up. You can also work hard enough that the boss needs to hire more workers thereby requiring another management position to be made available. As such you are first in line for the new management position. Keep that in mind when you decide how hard to work. Sometimes you simply need to create your own opportunities. Never wait for them to appear simply work so hard you create them.

CHAPTER 6

Increasing Your Skill Set: The Viable Approach

Ask yourself this question: "What is my skill set?"

If you had to sit down and write a list of your true skills, what would you list? Take a moment, grab a piece of paper, and list out all your skills that you think have any value to the marketplace whatsoever. Once you have that list, ask yourself, "Who would pay you to use these skills, and how much would they pay you to do it?" Now, for most of you reading this book, the sad reality is going to be that skill-set list is pretty short, and the value of those skills is pretty small, and the list of the people who would pay you to do those skills is also extremely small. People don't intend to not be good at stuff. People don't intend to not be valuable in their job, or in the world, but the sad reality of it is that that is where the vast majority of people live. I don't know if there are any statistics, but from my personal experience with the thousands of people that I have coached and the thousands of companies where I have trained, I can tell you right now that 90 percent of the people I worked with simply do not have a skill set that has any real value beyond minimum wage whatsoever.

So then by definition what they have is a "low skill" set. Now, I am sure some of you have heard of the term "low-skill worker." · e reality is the vast majority of people in the workforce are low-skill workers. What does that term mean, exactly? What is a low-skill worker? A low-skill worker is someone who has the skills of a starting position. I like to use McDonald's, Walmart, and Target as examples. You just need the basic High School level skills of arithmetic, writing, reading, and that is all you need at this job level. Now, of course, there is always some training involved, but that is typically no more than a week or two of remedial training of their systems or their point-of-sale systems or the inventory and how it works, and the employee manual your boss tells you to follow and where and who they are. Within two weeks, with your low skill set and a little amount of training, you are off and running in an entry level jobs at any of these types of companies. - is, unfortunately, is going to be something at which you cannot make much money, hence the term entry level.

Typically, the average low-skill full-time employee in the United States of America currently makes about $30,000 a year. I can tell you, $30,000 a year does not buy you much. You are looking at living a pretty low lifestyle if you are going to be willing to live off $30,000 a year. I'm sure you have heard the buzz term called "A living wage". Besides cunning politicians constantly using it I'm not sure what that even means exactly, and I don't think even the proponents of it understand exactly what it means. For arguments sake let us just say that it means you made enough to pay your rent, car payment, insurance, food, clothes. What would you have left in most American cities on $30,000 a year? - at's $2,500 per month, minus all monthly expenses. Take a couple of moments and add it all up, then throw in an extra couple of hundred a month for emergencies, odds and ends, and you could see the $2,500 a month does not go very far.

Matter of fact, it is the new American nightmare not the new American dream. Most people above 20 years old cannot make it on that kind of money anymore, unless you live in a very, very low-income area, where, unfortunately, your income will also be lower because they will pay lower in that lower-income area. So, the bottom line is that being a low-skilled worker and having a low-skill job is basically purgatory. Because as a low skilled worker you are going to be stuck in a bad job, in a bad neighborhood, in a bad apartment, driving a bad car with bad credit, and hoping to God that nothing happens between now and your next paycheck that you might cost a little extra money, like you need some new tires or something happens with your car, or there are some unexpected medical expenses that insurance would not cover. All these things happen to all of us all the time. Are you prepared? If you are a low-skill worker, I'm going to say NO.

So that is the problem. Now, why are more and more people losing the ability to climb above this level of pay? Why are they losing the battle of gaining high-income skill sets? Almost everybody who can read, write, and do basic arithmetic can be a low-skilled worker. You can make that $2,500 a month, but, unfortunately, again, that goes nowhere. So why are they missing the high skill set needed to make more income? Why are you missing a higher-income skill set? Ask yourself that question: Why are you missing it? Did someone not knock on your door and give it to you? Did someone not take you after high school to a special school and spend a year or two teaching you various high-income skill sets so that you could make $70,000–$100,000 a year? What happened to that class? Where was it? What happened to the people who were supposed to come and knock on your door and give you the higher income skill set? Guess what? · ey are not coming.

· ere is no special class. High school does not prepare you for anything except a low-skilled job, and, trust me, the people running the schools want you in that exact situation. You better understand something, and you better understand it well. · is world does not want you to be successful. · is system, even the greatest system in the world—the United States of America—does not want you to be successful. · ey want you to be low-skilled. · ey want you to make a low income because they want you to be dependent on the system. · at is the plan. "Make them need us. If they don't need us, then we can't keep the game going. As long as they need us, we can control them, dictate to them, make them follow rules, make them do what we want, vote for us, and so forth." It is sad, but it is the truth, and the better and the faster you learn it, the better off you are going to be.

So usually no one is coming for you to magically give you a high skill set that's the truth and it hurts. But if you are reading this book, congratulations! My knock on your door was heard, and you opened it, and here we are. So, guess what? I'm going to give you the way to get the high skill set no one else would. It is going to be me doing it for you not them who ever "them" ever was? Now, the price I am going to charge you is very high indeed! · e cost is your full attention. You have to pay attention and be willing to learn, spend some time, and a little amount of money eventually, and you have to want it. No one can make you want it. You have to want it for yourself. Nobody can teach you something you don't want to learn. · at is 90 percent of the problem. So, if you have this book in your hands, then hopefully I am talking to someone who does want to learn, because I can show you everything you need to know. You just have to want it. So if you are ready to make that commitment then let's get it done!

All right, let us get into it.

· e first rule about getting a high skill set—it is going to be the most valuable and it is that you have to learn to earn. Remember that phrase: "learn to earn." You have to learn before you can earn. It does not matter what job you are at, what you are doing, what education level you have, what color you are, what religion you believe in, or what God you pray to. · e bottom line is that you cannot earn more money until you acquire a high-level skill set. High-income skill sets do not come easy, and they do not come cheap. Most people cannot teach it to you. I have been doing this for over two decades, in that time I have been teaching people and business owners how to fix their skill sets so that they can increase their income, revenues, and grow sales.

· e good news is that it is not magic or something intangible in fact there is a formula. It is just like math: two plus two equals four. It equals four in the United States. It equals four in China. It equals four in Russia. It equals four on the Moon. It equals four on the other side of the Universe. · ere are universal principles that, when mastered, will assure you that you have a high level income skillset that will be able to generate you a high level of income over a sustainable period of time. Your first goal as part of this process, first and foremost, is to get your income up to a reasonable level. What is a reasonable level? At least $8,000 a month. · e first level you need to achieve is to get your earnings or net profit up to at least $8,000 a month or the $100,000 a year. · at is what you need to be chasing to launch this massive income growth process. Once you get that done, the world opens up to you. · ere is a magic to it. Once you can do that, then you can scale and continue to increase to $16,000; $24,000; $32,000; $50,000; $100,000 per month etc. · ere is no limit because now it is just a matter of scaling that skillset and its delivery to the marketplace. But there are challenging skills you have to acquire to be able to earn that first $8,000 a month, that is what you have to get, and you have to get them as fast as you possibly can.

Now I'm going to give you a few basic rules about how to acquire a high-income skill set. · e first is to understand the concept of high-income skills, which is simple if you break it down. · erefore, you simply need a skill that is worth roughly $40 per hour that you can deploy in the marketplace at roughly 200-220 hours per month. · e second rule is that you need to be the best in your space. Being the best at what you currently do is the very first thing that you can affect. I can teach you how to make $8,000 a month right now if you can simply be the best at your current skill set. So, in order to get there, here's what you have got to do. You have to be the best in your space. It doesn't matter what you are doing or what job you have right now; the first thing you have to do, if you want to get your high-income skill set, is to be the best in your space.

So, now, what does that mean? Well, if I'm a janitor, I'm going to be the best damn janitor there is. Period. So, the first thing I'm going to do to maximize my now is to say, "Okay, I'm a janitor. Now, I need to go get some knowledge on how to be a great janitor. I need to do some research. I need to raise my skills. For instance is there a better chemical that would make the floor shinier? Is there a technique that will help me to do the job more efficiently, faster, better? Is there something about the system I'm using to clean bathrooms and scrub toilets that needs to be improved? Is there a pumice bar instead of a bleach that would improve my results? All these things go into me being a great janitor."

It is called the tricks of the trade in layman's terms, and again, it is vital, if you ever want to get a high-income skill set. If you can't be the best janitor in the world, then what are you going to do beyond that? You have to be able to master the basics before you can master the masters. So, whatever you are doing right now, you have to be the best at it and that is a simple and fairly quick thing to get accomplished in most cases. How? First, refer to the 1% rule and apply! Second, let me teach you the "Power of 7".

What is the power of seven? It is the learning rule I use to make sure that I gain knowledge quickly and effectively. Simply it is making the commitment to dedicate seven hours a week to learning new skills and improving the ones you have. For instance, to get started YouTube is a fantastic resource. Hopefully by now, if you are reading this book, you have subscribed to my YouTube channel, and you know that I'm slinging out information and education for free on my channel. If you have not subscribed to it, this is a plug, go do it. Go do it right now. Lots of good stuff is going to help you there. · erefore, if you want to be a great janitor, you have to go study it, and YouTube is a great place to start. Next, take your phone for instance. How about you get off social media news feeds for a minute and instead get on some education websites. Get on some podcasts, Facebook coaching channels and learn how to be the best at what you are doing right now.

Next you should read books on the mastery of janitorial services. Read books on everything, really. Try to read three books a week, or even two books a week if you can. Of course, some of us don't have the time for that. But I always recommend that you read at least one book a week while your leaning your high-income level skill. Books will teach you how to become an expert at understanding your work product and environment and making the most of it.

You will see how fast you can improve in what you are doing. · e effect that this will have, of course, is who-ever you are working for is going to immediately appreciate you. · at is what we talked about in the previous chapters: the appreciation of your boss, the person you work for. Having that opens up a tremendous amount of opportunities. If you have proven to your boss that you are striving to be the best in your position—that you want to be the best in your space, whatever that may be—the boss is going to take notice. · at is where vertical movement can come in quickly and dramatic pay increases achieved.

Now, when you want a raise or a bonus, you can go to the boss and say, "Hey, you have seen how great a janitor I am. I want something more. What else can I do that you would be willing to pay me more for?" · e boss, now aware of the time and energy you spent to go be the best janitor in the world, is going to recognize that ambition and say, "Hey, I have another job that you can do. If you approach it the same way, dedicated to be the best in that space, I will give you a shot at this higher-level position." · is higher-level position will have a higher-level skill-set requirement, which means what? More money. You are starting to see the connection, I hope. So, the higher-level skills you acquire will equal higher pay.

· e next thing is that you have to make sure that you get a mentor and a coach. Now that you have this book, I hope I am at least one of those people for you. I think I am a pretty good mentor, and I know I am a hell of a coach. So, start with me. Expand, learn what I have to teach, then go from there and reach out to others. Nobody should have just one mentor and one coach. I have had countless. I don't know how many programs, packages, and trainings I have bought over the years or books I have read. I have long lost count. I have spent tens of thousands of dollars on mentoring programs, online training courses and books. · ere are lots of good coaches out there. · ey all have something and can add some value to your skill set. · ink about it. If you pay $1,000–$2,000 for a training course, and you learn a new skill that makes you $1,000 more a month, it has paid for itself in the first month alone. · e ROI on that thing was 1200 percent. You cannot lose if you are investing in something like that. Invest in yourself. · at is what you have to do. Now, you also have to be held accountable. You have to make sure that you are willing to be held accountable. It is all fine and dandy to talk the talk, but you have to be able to walk the walk.

Here is how I always suggest doing it. Hire an accountability coach or if money is tight to get started go to somebody you care about and someone who cares about you. You tell them, "Look, I want to be better. I want to make more money. I want to move better, be better, do better, provide better." · en, you add, "I want you to hold me accountable." Anytime they see you slipping, or wandering off track, you tell them, "Hey, you need to get me back on track. I want to be held accountable," and they will gladly get you back on track. Everyone can do it for someone else, but it is hard for us to do it for ourselves, right? But with someone to help you get back on track, it is easy. You just have to want it. So, do not be afraid to hold yourself accountable. It is vital. Once you get up to the $8,000 per month level that is when you need to get serious and hire a professional accountability coach. · en you will set yourself up to really get moving to the ultimate $42,000 per month that you need to achieve.

Another factor is you have to be willing to train in front of others. Now, I have hired, trained, and fired hundreds of people. One of the reasons I see a lot of people fail is they get stage fright. Look, you have got to get over it. You have to be willing to do whatever you have to do in front of others. We could all go in the backyard and play basketball and make some shots, but put us out there in front of fifty people and everybody starts to panic. You have got to get over that. · e easiest way to do it is to find a bunch of people and go do something that you have not mastered yet in front of them, and just get it out of your system that there is anything to be afraid of. As the famous saying goes, "· ere is nothing to fear but fear itself." · at holds true with training, learning new skills, speaking, public speaking, everything. · e fear is the biggest thing. · en, once you get used to it, you realize, "What was I afraid of?"

For example let's take public speaking, which I am committed to do more of. No matter how great of a public speaker somebody is, he or she is still working on it all the time. Nobody can master it. It is an unmasterable thing. Now you can be proficient, you can want to master it, you can work your whole life to master it, but it is always a work in progress. Life is a piece of art that is always a work in progress. It is never finished. You are always trying to make it better. · erefore, never be afraid to train, and later perform, in front of others it will make you better quicker than almost anything else.

· e last thing that goes into getting a high-income skill set faster is that you have to work harder. Let us face it. You have to put in the work. Michael Jordan, the greatest basketball player of all time, put in a lot of work, spending a lot of hours in that gym. He showed up early, stayed late, worked harder while he was there, putting more hours with greater intensity. Among all champions, that is always the hallmark mentality. · ere is nobody who has ever been a champion that someone said, "Yeah, that guy was kind of lazy. He showed up late. He left early. He kind of half-assed it while he was here." But he is a champion. You think so? Nope. Champions work harder, longer, and better because they know they have to get that high skill set as soon as possible. Michael Jordan had to get the high skill set. Tiger Woods had to get the high skill set and you'll need that high-income skill set as well. You have to work on it. Again, you are going to have to put in another ten to fifteen hours a week. Forty hours a week is nonsense. Get it out of your mind. We will talk about it in the later chapters about the time you really have to put in, but just know, for now, that forty hours is a joke. You have to put in fifty to fifty-five.

If you follow this simple, basic pattern, and hopefully there is nothing here that has been rocket surgery for you, you will see that by combining all those different facets, you will raise your skill set rapidly. Within a matter of days, your skills, knowledge, accountability, and courage will all increase.

No one rolled out of the womb great at something. It is all learned and trained, so you have to get going at it.

CHAPTER 7

Why Outside Influence Maflers

A major point that a lot of people miss in understanding how to do better in business and work is learning how to control their working environment. Now this may seem a little counterintuitive to what I said in an earlier chapter regarding not trying to control other people, but that does not mean that you cannot control your working environment. Now this takes a little amount of practice and understanding, but once you get it down, you will feel much more in control when it comes to your own work environment. A lot of people go to work and feel they are just a cog in a wheel with no participation and no ability to influence an outcome, and, unfortunately, that plays into a big part of the negativity we talked about in the previous chapters that then leads to 85 percent of people hating their jobs. You cannot ever get good at your job if you hate it. It just cannot happen. · erefore, understand that if you want to get good and increase your skill level, if you want to be happier and worth a higher income, you have to be able to learn how to control your working environment.

Now, as previously discussed, while you cannot control others, you can certainly control yourself. So how would that help you control your work environment? Very simply, by taking a different approach to your working environment it will allow you to influence the mentality of others, which will then circle back and create a better working environment for you. Better working environments are happier, more productive working environments. Now, this all begins, obviously, with ridding yourself of negativity. Now, I know it is not easy to do, but it is something you will have to learn how to master if you are going to be able to maximize your work environment.

·ere are some simple and very effective techniques to do so, and some of these you have heard before, so I am simply going to reiterate some basics that will make perfect sense and be easily followed. ·e most important thing about controlling negativity in your life is understanding where negativity originates. Most people want to believe that negativity originates from outside of themselves, that it is somebody else or some external force—the weather, the wind blowing, the rain, your boss or customer in a bad mood, your coworkers having a bad day etc. And of course whatever you believe to be true is very easy to manifest and hence make it true. In that regard if any of the above applies at your work, and I am sure it does, then their negativity can easily become your negativity. So, when you ask somebody how they are doing and they begin to complain, rarely does anyone say, "Oh, because I'm not getting the job done, I'm choosing to be in a bad mood." No. It is always "My boss is angry. My coworker is being a bitch. It is raining. ·e wind is blowing, and so forth." You can see how allowing these outside influences into your life can affect your work environment. You cannot allow it if you hope to maintain positivity at work.

So, the first thing to do to rid this negativity is to simply understand that none of it matters. It has nothing to do with what you are going to get done today, except that it is a challenge, and nothing else. By choosing to think of it that way you can make it a mental game, which will help you to flip the mental switch to understand that you do not need to accept their negativity as your negativity. Understand that negativity does not come from without; it comes from within. Do not let outside influence affect your mentality, thereby trashing your working environment. By accepting that bad circumstances are part of the universe will allow you to then not allow them to create negative thoughts for you that may jeopardize your productivity and your goals, thereby rendering you less valuable. · is is a key strategy that you have to employ. It is not easy, but it is a discipline that you need to master so practice and get one percent better at it everyday.

Another trick that works really, really well to rid negativity and to help control your work environment is to start your day with a goal. I call it "daily quantitative goal setting." It does not have to be a big goal; it just has to be something you can get done today that is going to make a big difference. Remember, we are no longer time driven or task driven; we are outcome driven. So now that you have a new mentality of being outcome driven, you want to start each day with a goal that is going to create a certain outcome. · us, the goal is the vision of the outcome. For instance, if I owned a fencing company and was performing fencing work for a client, I may decide that today I wish to get done eighty feet of fencing. · at is the goal. In doing so, you have made your goal quantitative. You also know that if you get the outcome of eighty feet of fencing, then obviously you are going to be able to meet that goal. Once you have the outcome of eighty feet of fencing today, you have done today's work. You had a specific goal, and you got the outcome needed. It doesn't matter how long or how short it took. Only that the goal was set and the outcome was reached no matter what.

Once today's work is done—and done well—you obviously feel good. You have a positive mentality. Your boss appreciates you. · e customer appreciates you. You can see where this goes. · e positive mentality that is created will help drive more goals, more happiness, and ultimately make you more valuable. So, remember, it is vital to start the day with a goal. What is today's outcome desired? · at is the goal. Now, drive it. Do everything you can to get it done that day.

Another key way that you can control your working environment and help to get your teammates and your coworkers extra excited is to actively instill purpose within them. Again, while I cannot control them, what I can do is I can ask them to be purposeful along with me. ·is is a technique I teach a lot of my clients, and it works very, very well. I tell them that if they feel the work environment is negative, what they should try to do is go to fellow employees, customers or to the boss, and say, "Hey, can you help me with a specific task that we are working on, today?" By doing so, the coworker or the boss will be very impressed that you are enlisting their help to get the goal done for the good of all.

·is display of a positive attitude builds a teamwork-oriented environment. It will show that you are willing to be flexible when it comes to getting things done, and it works really, really well when employees do this with their boss, who thinks the employee is going the extra mile to reach the goal for today. It is a very easy way to make the work environment much better, get your team working with you and increase the overall positive mentality of the work environment.

So far, we have talked about the inside influences of your work environment. Now, let us talk about the outside influences in your own life that will also affect your work environment. Who are you being influenced by? Now, I want you to make it a little exercise here. I want you to grab a piece of paper and a pen, and I want you to write down the top five people in your life who influence you. Do not make a distinction between good and bad. Simply note down the top five people who influence you good or bad. It can be parents, grandparents, children, sisters, brothers, friends, spouses, any and all of them. Once you have written it down, I want you to examine this list of people. I want you to ask yourself, "Would I want to exchange places with them, financially?" Not personally. Not their height, weight, or age etc. Only financially.

Now, if the answer is no on any of these people on this list, then you need to get those people out of your life as far as an influence. Now, it is not always easy, because some of these are your friends and family, your spouses, but you have to do it. Now, I am not saying that you should not love them, or spend time with them, but you have to cut them off as an influence. Do not take their advice, and do not consider their opinion; simply have fun with them, have some drinks on the weekends, go to a barbecues etc. Now, once you get the names off the list of the people who need to be eliminated, try to think of people you know with whom you would want to trade financial lives with.

Now, I want you to take those names and add them to your list in place of the ones you removed. ·ey could even be acquaintances, though it would be better if they are a little closer than that. No matter take it upon yourself to get to know them better. By surrounding yourself with five influential people whom you look to and trust for influence and mentorship, you will pull yourself up. ·eir insight will help you see and try di erent things. ·ey will make sure you are working on your skill set, and they will also hold you accountable, because they are not going to simply let you fail. ·ey are going to also look at you and say, "Well, if we are going to be associated with you, you better be trying to get to our level."

It is also very important to note that the five top people who influence you most are going to be the ones whom you decide. So, it is important, very important, I can't stress it enough, you have got to choose the five people who influence you the most by making sure that you'd be willing to trade finances with each and every one of them. If the answer is no, then they cannot be allowed to be one of your five influencers. If you follow this advice to create your personal influencer list, you will find that your work environment will improve, coworkers will treat you better, customers will respect you more, the boss will look upon you more favorably, you will be more productive, and the results will absolutely be measurable.

Never underestimate the power of outside influence. It can be one of the biggest keys to your overall success.

CHAPTER 8

Playing the Political Game at Work

Let's face it, politics is always going to be a part of work environments. It is just how it is. It is how human beings are programmed. We are cliquish. We learned this in school obviously; whoever looks like us, walks like us, and talks like us becomes a part of our little clique. Because of this tendency, we form little tribes within any organization, whether it be a school or the work environment.

So, what can you do to deal with the people in your environment that do not wish to include you in their clique? Like everything else in the universe, this is beyond your control. · erefore, instead of trying to wish for them to be different or being angry or negative about them being different, let us just say they are different. It is what it is. But let us tailor our approach to make sure we are successful despite the challenges.

In this chapter, we are going to learn about how to masterfully play the political game at work. I am sure you have been the victim of politics in the work environment, from nepotism to simply being overlooked for a position to downright hatred and animosity. One of the first things you need to understand, if you are going to master the political game at the office or at your work, is that even if you are not in the same clique as your superiors they are not the bad guys. · ere is a general perception—I am sure it is shared by many —that bosses are mainly evil and want to whip you into compliance. · ey want to demean you. · ey want to walk all over you, use you, step on you. However, it is simply not true. You have to look at it from the boss's perspective. ·e boss needs you to be successful. If you are not successful, it reflects negatively on the boss.

So, for the boss to wish that you were not successful, or that you did not have a good working environment, would simply be to wish for their own destruction. I don't know about you, but there are not a lot of us in the work environment who are hoping for our own destruction, and it certainly is not your boss. ·e reason why they have climbed to the station above you is because they clearly have some type of ambition, goal orientation, and reasonable ability to get the job done. Otherwise, they would not be in that position. · erefore, understand the boss is not the bad guy.

Now, they don't always communicate this properly, and I think that is where a lot of this comes from. · is can be attributed to poor communication skills, and it makes the boss look like they are simply demanding and demeaning and looking to badger you into compliance. · is would certainly make them look bad, but, in reality, this is simply their lack of ability to communicate properly their true desire and wishes to have you succeed, thereby helping them be successful in their position as well.

So, the next time you interact with your boss, remember that your boss actually has great intentions when it comes to your success. Do not think the boss is out to get you. Just understand the boss is, perhaps, a poor communicator and even a little insecure. With this newfound power, you will have the ability to get past the surface and the perceptions of slights and insults from your boss, and understand the true, underlying desire, which is for everyone to be successful. · is will unleash your ability to move freely in your work environment without having any animosity or mistrust of your boss. · is is vital, if you want to master the political game at work and get the most out of your work environment.

Next, in the political spectrum at work, come your colleagues and coworkers. Now, again, as high school was with cliques, groups, and tribes forming within the class, we see animosity and mistrust among co-workers. Now with co-workers yes sometimes, they do not have your best interests in mind and are out to get you. · is is a fact. Sometimes, they are competing for your job. Sometimes, they are beneath your station and wish for your job. Other times, they simply believe that your elimination or failure will either make them look better or will help propel them to the next level. Either way, you are right to be skeptical of some of the motives of your colleagues and coworkers, because they do not always have your success in mind.

Often, envy can lead them to actually wish you to fail, even if it may damage them as well, because as the team goes, so does the individuals. If the company is not profitable, they certainly cannot afford to give raises or promotions to the employees. So, while your colleagues might simply just not be smart enough to understand the ramifications of their wishes, some of them may wish you ill will. · e question is, what to do about it?

· e first thing to do, which is like everything else in the world, is to fully understand what the situation is. Like everything else I have talked about previously, there are some things you cannot control; you certainly cannot control the thoughts, ideas, and intentions of your coworkers. · erefore, like anything else, simply understand that it is what it is, and make the proper adjustments to control what you can control, which is, in fact, you. · erefore, the way to handle any coworkers you don't get along with or certainly don't have your best interest in mind is to simply wrap your brain around the fact that this is how it works and to really not pay much attention to it. It is better to simply ignore it and move about your business, your day, and your goals, instead of worrying about or spending any valuable emotional energy focusing on colleagues and coworkers that do not have your best interest in mind.

Simply smile to them, and pay them no further attention; instead of believing that they are undermining your success, as they will not be because you are now empowered with the ability to ignore their attempts to sink your ship. Instead, simply refer to the positive mind-set of understanding that you came into work today with a goal. Do not allow them to distract your goals. If you simply focus on your goal, you cannot help but be successful.

Your colleagues and coworkers are usually easily avoidable, but in the rare cases where you actually need the colleagues and coworkers to help complete tasks, the best way to go about it is by simply smiling, giving them a compliment, and telling them that you would make sure they are going to be successful as well because as you go, they will go.

I would even drop it in there that you tell them you will give a good word to the boss about their contribution to the outcome of this goal. · at will at least spur them to have a more positive mentality with you, so they would be happier to help. · us, it is better to outsmart them than it is to attempt to beat them at their own tactics and games. Simply move around them or move over them, but do not let them take you down. · at is the rule.

· e other parties that are involved in the political game at work, of course, are customers. Now, we all know the old adage that the customer is always right. Well, as you already know that is not true. Customers are not always right, but let me make one thing really clear: customers are the real Boss. What does that mean? It means the customers have the final say. Customers and clients will either decide to spend money with you or not, and there is not much you can do about it if they choose not to, so the key is to again understand that there are things beyond your control. · ere are still ways to be successful, despite the fact that you cannot control customers directly. Instead, make your control, and influence over customers more indirect, and you will find that it is not only more successful but also avoids the pitfalls, stresses, and negativity that can come with an argument with a customer over a point that really does not matter.

I will give you a prime example of a customer interaction that could be handled either directly or indirectly, with regard to a dissatisfied customer. Let us say that you are a waiter at a fine restaurant, and the customer there has a complaint about the steak. · e customer says that the steak is too tough, and they are not happy with it, and therefore, they do not want to pay their bill. Now, you could argue with the customer and tell them that the steak was delicious, soft, and juicy, and they are simply either lying because they don't want to pay or they are simply too stupid to understand what a good steak is. Now, while this may be accurate, it will not work to keep the customer happy, and the customer will either not pay this bill or will never come back again, thereby taking future sales away from you and your organization.

So, what is the right way to handle this? How do you still win in that situation? Well, let me tell you. No matter the customer's complaint, whether it is real or perceived, the fact is that it has to be dealt with. · e best way I have ever found to deal with complaining or dissatisfied customers is to simply ask them for their feedback. So, instead of saying they are wrong or their feelings don't matter, say something like this instead: "Please tell me, Mr. Johnson, why was the steak not up to your standards?" · e customer, at that point, would then have to give you specifics as to why the steak was not satisfactory. Now, again, I'm not going to argue with the customer about what their standards are. I will simply acknowledge that we have missed the mark on this one, but we would be happy to make up for it.

I would then ask Mr. Johnson what he believes is a fair compensation to make up for the lack of a quality product in his eyes. Most of the time, they will give you some reasonable explanation, or, sometimes, they will ask for no discount. Sometimes, they will simply say, "Well, I don't want any compensation for this. I just wanted to let you know, and I appreciate the fact that you didn't disregard my opinion." A lot of times, just listening to the complaint and understanding it for what it is—an emotional response—is enough for the customer to feel satisfied that they were listened to, their complaint was recognized, and because you fielded it properly, the customer has no animosity toward you or the company and will happily pay their bill and come back, especially if they know that you are fully committed to making sure that the next time they visit, you will go above and beyond to meet their expectations.

Now, on the rare occasions where a customer is simply trying to run a scam by either not paying the bill or getting something for free, that is unreasonable. Obviously, that has to be dealt with. · at is rare, but it does happen. · e best way to deal with it is to simply ask the customer why they feel the need to not pay the bill. If the customer has justification in not paying the bill, then you obviously give them a credit or a discount. If the customer has no justification but still demands the discount, simply accept. Even if you have to lose money and lose the customer, it is better than empowering the customer with the fact that you did not meet their satisfaction, allowing them to run out and file complaints on the internet, where they could bash you on websites like Yelp, Google, and others.

· erefore, what you want to do is to simply avoid this by making them at least moderately satisfied with the outcome. It does not mean that you have to be victimized by these people. It simply means it is better to lose now than to lose later. Lose a little now, save a lot later, and understand who they are, and no longer seek business from them ever again. Send them on their way, thank them, and the next time, simply tell them you are not available to service them. After a couple of times of that, such customers will usually take their business elsewhere. · e truly dishonest customer will be few and far between.

Overall, the best way to play the political game at work, whether you are dealing with bosses, coworkers, or customers, is to always move with their best interest in mind. Always smile, be reasonable, polite, professional, and courteous, and speak and act such that they believe you are looking after their best interest, whether it is in your best interest or not is irrelevant. It will reflect positively upon you and will allow you to have a greater influence over these people and therefore create a better outcome.

If the person believes that you have their best interest at heart then when it comes time for you to give them advice on how to handle something, do something, complete a task, and so forth; they will have a much more favorable opinion and outlook of you, and, thereby, there will be a much greater chance for them to comply. Understand that playing the political game means that you are going to have to overcome the small things that would otherwise hold you back with regard to people's complaints, lack of willingness to cooperate with you, and/or general animosity or envy. What you have to do, instead, is move with the best intent in mind, thus giving you control and influence over these people to have the power to create a better outcome.

Also, it will create a mind-set for you of positivity, instead of negativity, whereby you would be able to stay on task so that you can meet your goal for the day. Moving in this way is going to help you tremendously in maintaining a positive outlook as well as making sure that you are able to influence and move people around you in the best way possible for your own success. Always understand it all comes back to you. You will be more successful if you play the political game well at work. It is not hard. You just have to understand how to make sure you can take advantage of all those situations.

· e second thing to do is to ensure hard work is seen as your identity. What does that mean exactly? It means that everyone who perceives you, whether it is your boss, a coworker, a colleague, or a customer, their general perception of you should be that you are a hard worker. Now, don't try to fake it until you make it. Make sure you simply work hard every day, work well, and work with other people's best interests in mind. If hard work is your identity, you will find that it very quickly translates into much greater benefits for you.

It also decreases envy from coworkers and elicits their cooperation in meeting tasks. · e boss's view of you is that you are one of his best and favorite workers and that you can always be relied upon to get a solid day's worth of work done. · is will encourage the boss to communicate with you about possibilities for promotions and raises, as well as the fact that you will be first in line regarding any benefits or other general intangibles around the office.

I cannot stress it enough. Having your identity be that of a hard worker is imperative if you wish to be successful in your career.

·e next and last thing to be mindful of in playing the political game at work is pride. Now, pride is a double-edged sword. On the positive side pride can make you very successful. It can hold you accountable. It can make you work harder, make you be more responsible, and make you do right by others. However, pride can also destroy you. It is very important that you understand the differences. Most people, unfortunately, don't always let pride help them. Most people allow pride to destroy them. ·ey do so because they allow what they perceive to be insults, slights, and general negativity in their direction affect them to the point that their ego is damaged.

·eir response to that is to lash out, be negative, do less work and not more, be less goal-oriented instead of more, and have terrible productivity. I have watched pride destroy more companies and careers than any other single thing that I know. Pride, while it can be a very positive thing, more often than not serves as a means of destruction. Do not let your pride get in the way. Do not allow your pride to make you become negative. Do not allow your pride to make you think less of others or want to try less. Simply understand that your pride cannot be injured unless you let it.

Make sure that your pride remains in check. Put it in your back pocket more times than not so that you cannot be insulted by somebody else. You cannot be made negative by somebody else, and despite how you perceive your boss or a difficult customer they should not affect your pride. Again, genuine insults are quite clear and are very rare. Perceived slights, which can be quite common in the workplace, are a perceived assault on your pride. Don't allow them to affect you. Keep your pride under control, and only use it for power, not for negativity.

As long as your pride does not get in the way, a lot of things that happen at work will simply roll off your back. Remember, it is better to have a thick skin and move with intent and purpose than it is to have thin skin and let little insults and perceived slights injure your pride to the point that you become negative and destructive. Let the small stuff roll off your back. You will be much better off for it, I guarantee you.

CHAPTER 9

Work Ethic and Why It Maflers Most

Effort. Give more effort.

How many times have we heard this in our lives? We hear it as children in grade school, middle school, high school, college, and beyond. Effort. An A for effort is what they say in school. He got an A for effort.

Obviously, we put a large emphasis on the word "effort." Because it means a lot. Even if you don't succeed at something, if somebody says you got an A for effort, you take pride in that. It means you tried really hard, and you gave it everything you had. So, again, how important is effort? It is the required ingredient for any and all success. Effort and work ethic matter more than anything else.

If you don't do a single other thing, understand that at least 70–80 percent of your success is going to be through work ethic and effort alone. I cannot overstate this and most understate it because it's hard and requires discipline. Understand that if you want the best of anything you have to give maximum effort. When do you do that? All day. What days? Every day. · ere are no days off for effort and work ethic when it comes to your goals. If you are going to take days off from your effort and your work ethic, you are going to lose and fall short of your goals. I can tell you that right now, point-blank.

You cannot give half your effort and expect to win. I don't care how smart, talented, or well-intentioned you are; if you do not work your full ass off, you are going to lose. It is just that simple. Again, like many other things in this universe, success is something you cannot control by hope or desire. The reality of it is that the world and the universe by default do not want you to succeed. The natural state of the universe is one of balance. What does this mean? It means that the universe wants half of the beings to be winners and the other half losers.

So, if the universe wants half of us to win, then it also wants half of us to lose. Now, do you want to leave your success at a 50/50 chance? Don't let the universe make this decision for you because those that do fall into the loser's half by default. If you wish to win, you have to say, "I'm not going to be placed where the universe wants me to be I'm going to choose to be in the winning half and this is what the universe is really looking for, the strong, those with the will to win, that's who the universe wants to win." So, tell yourself "I'm going to be one of the winners." So, what goes into that winning most? Work ethic! The universe loves those that put in the work. The universe rewards work and effort and punishes laziness and complacency. If you look around you can see this everywhere with your own eyes.

There has never been a champion at anything—at sports, business, or any profession—who has ever won without an amazing work ethic. From Einstein to Michael Jordan to some of our greatest political figures, nobody won without an amazing work ethic. It is simply not possible. Those who outwork others win, and those who underwork lose. It is as simple as that. Work beats talent every day and twice on Sundays! When it comes to the "why" in effort, so who are you supposed to do it for? In your work environment, whether you own a business or work for someone else, there is always a boss and a customer. Sometimes, the boss is the customer, and, sometimes, the customer is the boss. Either way, you have to give your maximum effort for those that you are trading your goods or services to for money if you hope to maximize the money you receive. Less effort equals less money for you.

You also have to give effort so that your colleagues and coworkers will look upon you favorably. Again, I cannot overstate how vital it is to be perceived by your coworkers, boss, and customers as being the hardest working person there is. You simply have to make it your calling card. It is necessary to maximize your position and hence your compensation.

Now, to help out with this, as far as wrapping your brain around it, I have come up with a little theory I call the "· irteen Boxes · eory." · e · irteen Boxes · eory is extremely simple like most successful things are. Overcomplicating things and making things too fancy does not make it more successful or more productive. Matter of fact, it often makes things unsuccessful and even counterproductive. So, I always like to keep everything that I teach simple and to the point.

· e · irteen Boxes · eory is simply as follows:

Let's say you get hired at a company as an employee or you own the business are hired by a customer to stack boxes, and the boss or customer tells you, "I would like you to stack at least twelve boxes a day. If you stack twelve boxes a day for us, we will consider that a solid day's worth of work, and we will pay you the amount we have contractually agreed upon for you to stack those twelve boxes."

Now, I can assure you, having been an employer for over twenty years, when told to stack twelve boxes, most employees stack eleven at best, and some only stack ten or nine. More times than not—I would say it is probably around 99 percent—the employee or contractor will actually stack fewer boxes than the daily agreed upon requirement. · is only ensures that that employee or business is destined to fail. Clearly, if the boss or customer wants you to stack twelve, and you are instead stacking ten, what will be your boss or customers perception of you? · e boss or customer is going to be upset, because now it reflects negatively and damages the boss or customer. Now you have a boss or customer that is going to complain for your not meeting the quota, which, of course, if you don't understand the political game of work, you are going to perceive as being some type of insult upon you. And, if you allow your pride to get involved, you can obviously see where that takes you.

· is is the scenario I see that happens far too often in the work environment to both employees and business owners. Instead, understand that your boss or customer simply is just not a good communicator. · ey are not going to be able to communicate with you as effectively as you would like the fact that you are failing their expectations and you need to stack twelve boxes and not eleven as you originally agreed. · is dynamic ruins more opportunities than any other factor.

Now, how can this be avoided? Simple. · e · irteen Box · eory. Remember the name of the theory is the · irteen Box · eory, not the Twelve Box · eory. So, to counteract this slippery slope, which occurs with 99 percent of all employees and businesses in the work environment. · erefore, instead of stacking eleven boxes, or even the twelve that is your expected quota, try this trick: stack thirteen! Instead of stacking one less, stack one more. Now, what will be the perception of your boss, customers, coworkers, and colleagues about you then?

Not only did you meet the quota but also you went above and beyond. You stacked thirteen boxes where others stacked eleven. You stacked thirteen boxes where the quota is only twelve. Now, you can quickly understand what this would create for you in the work or business environment. · e boss and customer would look upon you as a hard worker, your colleagues would look on you as someone who is more than pulling their weight, and their perception of you would be favorable, and the customers would be delightfully impressed and have a strong desire to buy more and give you ringing endorsements. Clearly, you can see that stacking thirteen boxes instead of twelve creates an immediate positive change to everybody's perception toward you.

What does this lead to? It leads to better sales, raises, promotions, accolades, and awards, and a much happier work environment to boot. · e power of stacking thirteen boxes instead of twelve is exponential in nature, leading to opportunities for more and larger contracts, rapid advancement, more money, and a higher station and explosive growth.

Simply stack thirteen, not twelve. And under absolutely no circumstances can you ever stack as much as your coworkers or competitors do, which is eleven. Always outwork them. · at has got to be your calling card. Understand the power of outworking everyone in your space. It proves to everyone that you are the one who can be counted on to get the job done and as such you will be rewarded. It is an absolute must.

Let us say, for a moment, that your job is not as simple as stacking boxes. It is not that simple and as tangible. Let us say that your job is nothing that has a quota-driven system. Let us say you are a medical worker. Let us say that you are providing a service for somebody and the service really cannot be counted in hard numbers. So, what would you do then? How would you guarantee that you would go above and beyond to make sure your work ethic and effort are always impeccable so you get that proverbial A for effort?

Well, just simply remember this: Go above the call of duty. Whatever you are asked to do, whatever you are supposed to do, just do a little extra. · e idea behind the · irteen Boxes · eory is simply this. Do 5–10 percent more than you were expected to. Do 10 percent more than you were asked. No matter what you are there to do, just do a little more, a little better, a little faster, with a slightly wider smile on your face. Just make it more. · at is the crux of this theory. · is will prove to everyone that you have an amazing work ethic and that you always get an A for effort, and regardless of the outcome, you always have proven that you are there to contribute and to win, and you can be counted on.

Another powerful theory as well that really impacts work ethic is the "Needs · eory". · is is much simpler but just as powerful. It's simply to just make sure that you are always putting others' needs above yours. What does that mean? It means that you need to accept self-sacrifice when necessary. If it comes down to someone else's needs versus your own, make sure their needs are met first, even if your needs are not met at all. If you do this in the work environment, again the perception will be that you are a team player and a winner, you have a high level of work ethic and effort, and that is going to translate into greater opportunities from employment and from customers for you.

Again, it all plays back into the power of perception. ·e power of the perception of people about you is everything. Let us face it; no matter what you want in this world, someone else has it. In order to get what you want, you are going to have to go to someone else, and they are going to have to give it to you. If you try taking it, that is called stealing, and obviously, there are consequences for that. · erefore, we are not going to steal. We want people to not only be willing to give us what we want but literally want to give us what we want and be thrilled to do so. Personally, I want my customers to want to give me more money, and my bosses to want to give me raises and promotions. Once in a while, you see these stupid sayings on the internet. "I don't care what people think," they say. · at is the most asinine and ignorant thing I have ever heard. · ink it through, if I make their perception of me negative, do you really think they are going to give me what I want very easily? Of course not. · ey are going to not want to give it to me at all let alone easily.

So yes, you should care what other people think of you. Of course, you do. Stop sharing the memes on the internet, saying, "I don't care what people think." · at means that you don't want yourself to do well. Never wish for yourself to do poorly. You absolutely should care about what other people think of you. Recognize it, acknowledge it, and live with that in the front of your mind. · ere is nothing wrong with it. It is the way to guarantee that you are going to win and that you are going to get what you want from those that have it.

·e key here is that the perception of others is always going to be your greatest tool in order to get what you want. If the perception of everyone you do business for and with is that you are there to help them, even at a sacrifice to yourself, imagine the power that has in getting those people to give you what you want. If you want more money from your boss, then show your boss you are self-sacrificing and put their needs above yours. If you want another order or a higher contract from your customer, then if you put their needs before yours, they are going to be inclined to give you what you want. So, the power of perception of others is instrumental in your success.

·e final theory I want to convey when discussing work ethic and effort, is the "Lucky ·eory". Let's discuss how luck plays into all of this as far too many people are waiting for old "luck" to always kick in to save them. So, let's take that into account. How does luck matter and how can it affect your job and your work environment? We've all heard, at least occasionally phrases like, "Oh they didn't work for it, they got lucky", "Better to be lucky than good."

Well, what is this magic power of luck exactly? Let us use the example of a sale that happened for us that we were not counting on, the unexpected purchase that was made, the car that got bought by the customer who happened to just wander in, and we conclude that the salesperson involved in those just got lucky. Well, let me tell you something about luck. Luck is mostly self-created. As I discussed the universe wants everything to be balanced. So, the universe does not believe in luck or at least good or bad luck. But if it does believe in luck, it believes in just as much bad luck as it does in good luck, so that luck becomes again 50/50, because the nature of the universe is to balance itself out.

·erefore, understand that if you think someone was lucky, you have to understand that the universe wants someone else to be unlucky. Now, in my opinion, I believe you create your own luck, and I have always taken it upon myself to control my own luck and not let the universe make that decision for me, because if I let the universe control my luck, it is going to give me just as much bad luck as it does good luck, and what is the net result going to be? Back to where I started at zero.

Knowing that is not what I want I must take control of my own luck. Now, what I do to create my own luck is that I simply increase my effort. Again, this all goes back to effort and work ethic. As a matter of experience, I have noticed that I have always gotten a lot luckier by working harder. A simple example of this would be that of flipping a coin. A coin has two sides heads and tails. We can call heads "good luck" and we can call tails "bad luck". Now how effort effects luck let's say I get paid for all the heads that come up. If I need a certain number of heads to come up when I'm flipping a coin, the more often I flip the coin, the more heads I am going to get. Now, in the end, it tends to reach 50/50, but if I get paid money for each head that comes up, the faster I flip the coin, the more heads I am going to get. · at is how you can create your own luck at work.

So, again, if I want a certain sale, a job, a promotion, or a raise, if that is luck, well, then I'm going to create it. So always move with the intent of creating your own good luck by controlling how many times heads will come up in a given period of time. Always work harder, faster, and better. Always keep increasing your skills. · is will give you the ability to get more heads in any given period of time such as a day, week, month or year.

You can also get lucky more often by showing up. I'm sure you have heard the saying, "Showing up is half the battle." Yes, it is. What exactly does that mean? Showing up means being present and actively contributing. Stack thirteen boxes, not twelve. You are going to get lucky because that extra box is the extra head on the coin I get paid for. · e more boxes you stack, the greater the chance you have to get the side of the coin that rewards you. · e more work you get done, and the more people you sell to, communicate with, and are appreciated by, the greater the chance for good luck to kick in. · at is how you create your luck. · ose things are what matters the most when it comes to getting "lucky".

Make your effort and work ethic your calling card. You have to be the hardest working person in the room. It is something you can always control; 100 percent of the time and it will lead to much great success in all you do.

CHAPTER 10

Providing Value to the Marketplace to Increase Your Pay

As we have already learned in the earlier chapters, there are two things that are always going to determine how much money you make: First is the amount of time you spend doing something, and the second is the rate at which you get paid to do it.

Consider the following example pay chart:

$10 an hour × 40 hours = $400
$10 an hour × 50 hours = $500
$12 an hour × 40 hours = $480
$12 an hour × 50 hours = $600

· us, you can see that the amount of money you make is always determined by the amount of time worked multiplied by the rate of pay. · e equation mathematically is simple: X times Y = Z, where X is the rate of pay and Y is the time worked then Z is the amount of money made.

Now, adding more time is simple. You just have to do it. Wake up earlier, arrive at work earlier, and stay later. Work more days. Take less time off. Controlling the (Y) time worked is simple.

⋅e second factor (X) is the rate of pay. Now, that is the trickier part, because the rate of your pay from minimum wage to $500 per hour, and everything in between, is going to directly depend on the value you are supplying to the marketplace. Write it down, and remember it. "⋅e value that I supply to the marketplace equals the rate (X) I get paid."

It has nothing to do with your boss, the company you work for, the economy, the president, politics, the weather, none of that. Get outside variables out of your mind. It is a myth. A lot of people want to believe that what they get paid depends on what the company is willing to pay them or some outside factor they cannot control. ⋅at is absolutely not true, and let me tell you why.

What determines how much an employer or customer will pay you for your work is based upon the fact that they want to pay as little as possible to get a particular job done or problem solved. Now, you cannot fault them for this. It is just natural that we all want the most stuff for as cheap as we can reasonably get it. We all want to pay the minimum that is required to get the job done. You do it as well. If your car breaks down and you take it to the mechanic, you want to get it repaired, and you want to get a quality repair, but you also want to get it at the least cost as you can. ⋅is is just basic economics, and it is no one's fault. Your employer or customer wants to get the job done at a reasonable level of quality for the cheapest price possible. ⋅e fact that you are doing your job for that price, and you are doing a good job means it is possible. ⋅is is neither your boss's fault nor the company's. ⋅e free market controls the price and it does it in a simple way. Price is set by the quality of the work given and the size of the problem it solves. As you might not be able to control the size of the problem right now to increase your rate of pay let's focus mostly on what you can control immediately, which is the quality of effort you provide.

First Rule on quality: You have got to become an expert at what you do. Remember, this book is about maximizing your now. So, whatever it is you are doing right now—whether you are a janitor, a schoolteacher, a plumber or a brain surgeon —the first thing you need to do to increase the value of what you are worth is increase your value to the marketplace via the quality of the work and the size of the problem it solves. For example - if you are a janitor, become an expert janitor. If you are a brain surgeon, become an expert brain surgeon. No matter what you do, become the best at it there is. · is will guarantee that the goods or services you provide are of the highest quality available, which will raise the value.

Second Rule on quality: Never expect something for nothing. Now, this is something that you really have to wrap your brain around, because it is a little tricky. Never expect something for nothing, which means that if you are looking to get something from someone, it cannot be with you doing nothing. You cannot go to your boss and ask for a raise because you are you. You cannot go to your customer and say, "Hey, I'm going to raise the prices because, well, I feel like raising the prices." · at is expecting something for nothing. It does not work, and it really upsets the marketplace. And the marketplace will not tolerate it well and certainly will not pay you more.

When you enter Walmart and you see a bunch of the prices, they will all say, "Reduced. Reduced. Reduced. Was $2, now $1.97." Why? Because the customer will become upset if a sign said, "Was $2, now $2.07." · at would cause the sales to decline because Walmart is asking for something more for no increase in value.

So, whenever you go to a customer or your boss and you want something, always be willing to offer something in return for higher pay: extra value, extra service, extra upgrade, more work, more time, better quality of work. · ere is always something more that you can offer. You have to exchange something for something, and the more perceived valuable your something has, the easier it is to get the higher pay you want.

· ird Rule of quality: Always under promise but overdeliver. What does that mean? Be very, very careful of what you promise. Never promise something you cannot do, and never make a promise you don't intend to keep.

· at is the surefire way to create a disaster. If you promise your boss you are going to work extra this week, you better do it. Don't promise it and not deliver. If you promise a customer you are going to get something done by Friday at three o'clock, don't come up short. If you come up short, you are going to get blowback. · e customer is going to be upset, and they will either want a discount, or not use you again in the future or worse not pay you at all.

For instance, if I promised that I would have it done by three o'clock on Friday, guess what? I am going to overdeliver. I am going to have it done by two o'clock on Friday. · en I will call my boss or my customer, and I will say, "Oh, that thing I promised you at three? Guess what? It is two, and I have it done." You don't have to overdeliver by hours and hours or days. Just beat it a bit. Just do a little more, that 10% more. It makes a big difference. Your customers, your boss, and everyone in your workplace will think more of you because of it, which will increase your quality and hence value to the marketplace.

Fourth Rule of quality: Make sure you are results driven. We have talked about this in the previous chapters, but it cannot be overstated. Make sure the results your boss or your customer wants are produced without fail. If the boss wants twelve widgets delivered by three, either have twelve widgets delivered by two or have thirteen widgets delivered by three. Never come up short. Always guarantee your results, and live up to those guarantees.

Fifth Rule of quality: Always maintain the highest ethics and integrity. If you want to increase your value to the marketplace, the people you do business with have to believe that you are a person of high ethics and integrity. It is always going to increase your quality and value. If people perceive you as being highly ethical and someone having tremendous integrity, they will be willing to spend more money with you as a customer. · ey will be willing to place more orders and larger orders. Your boss will be willing to give you more raises, bonuses, and promotions if they know that you are a person of high ethics and integrity.

Sixth Rule of quality: Make sure you are prepared for unforeseeable circumstances. · is kind of goes contrary to other factors. · ere are always issues that come up. It is just a part of life. It is unavoidable. You have to fix the things that can affect the quality of what you are providing. When something unavoidable and catastrophic does happen, you have to assure your customers, boss, and coworkers that you will mitigate it and find a solution.

Unforeseeable circumstances can affect the promise of the delivery. If you cannot keep the promise of the delivery, you have to be honest and forthcoming about it, and, most importantly, you have to promise to fix it. · is will preserve the perception people have of you even in the event you cannot keep your original agreement for the work.

Don't try to avoid it, or act like it didn't happen. Acknowledge it, and promise to fix it. It will work in your favor. People will understand. It will actually work to make you more valuable. People will pay you more, the boss will understand, and you will still get the promotion and the raise. So, make sure to always acknowledge and fix the unforeseeable problems.

Seventh Rule of quality: Hold yourself accountable. · is entire list will not matter if you don't hold yourself accountable to it. If you allow yourself to make excuses, your quality and hence value will go lower instead of going higher. Instead of people paying you more, they would want to pay you less. Instead of getting a raise, you might get a demotion or a pay cut. · e customer will come back less, order less, and pay less. If you don't hold yourself accountable, it will lower your value to the marketplace.

People who get paid more do so because they are worth more, because they are experts at what they do. · ey under promise and overdeliver. · ey never expect something for nothing. · ey always produce results. · ey are persons of high ethics and integrity. When unforeseeable things do happen, they promise to fix them. And they always hold themselves accountable. Today you can control the quality of work you provide following these seven rules.

Once you have mastered the quality of work you provide you can then turn your focus on solving a larger problem.

· is is the easy part. Simply understand that controlling the size of the problem for (X) just means a solution to a larger problem. Whether that is simply by selling the customer 100 widgets instead of 50 or if your boss wants you to take on a more important role at the company. To increase your rate is as simple as doing a larger job for the customer or doing a more important task for your employer either because you accept more responsibility or because you got a promotion to a higher position. Clearly the manager of a restaurant will make a higher hourly rate than the dishwasher due to the increased responsibility. By controlling the quality of the work product, you provide you can more times than not automatically increase the size of the problem your boss or customer is willing for you to solve, thereby increasing your rate of pay.

CHAPTER 11

Proper Work-Time Management

· is is often overlooked by most people. While we have talked about how you should not ever be time driven and be results driven instead, obviously, time as a living breathing thing still plays a major role if you want to be successful.

You have to be able to manage your work time to dedicate the necessary resources and efforts to achieve your desired result. As most of you already know, the more time you put in, the more you get out. · at applies the same to many things in life such as the gym, reading, learning, studying, everything. It is the same for working as well. · e less you put in, the less you get out. It is a simple mathematical equation.

Of course, "time in" does not mean you just should sit there and watch the clock tick away without getting anything done, because then the time will become valueless.

When it comes to work, your time can be worth either $10 per hour, $100 per hour, or $500 per hour. · e time's value is dependent upon what you get done during those periods.

· at said, if I make my time be worth $500 per hour, for every hour I put in, I get another $500. Ten hours of work would earn me $5000 and I'm sure you would admit that is a lot of money. · erefore, proper work-time management is vital if you want to be results driven and increase your rate of pay. I will give you the rules as follows.

First Rule: In early, out late. What does that mean? It means that you need to get to work early, and you need to stay late. If work is supposed to start at 8:00 a.m. and continue till 5:00 p.m., you need to get in at 7:00 a.m. and work till 6:00 p.m. You must have heard the adage, "·e early bird gets the worm." ·at is absolutely true. ·e universe rewards those who get in earlier. Birds and animals that get out earlier to hunt have a better chance at survival and are more prosperous. ·e same works for humans as well. If you get up early, get to work early, and make more of your day, you are going to be more prosperous. Again, it goes back to the self-creation of good luck we discussed previously. More activity is going to equal more good luck, which leads to opportunity for more production, and therefore more money. ·ese are basic rules of the universe. ·ey apply to everything, including your work time.

Second Rule: Forget the forty-hour workweek. We have all been told a full-time job is forty hours, and we are now accustomed to it, but it is a scam, and here's why. If I want greater production and greater results then of course I can increase both by adding more time not less time. However, getting more production out of less time is also always the goal. However, at some point, putting in a lack of time not only becomes detrimental to the ability to get sufficient production accomplished it also robs you of being able to gain greater skills and hence be able to produce more value in any given period of time.

I will give you a simple real-world example of what I mean.

Let's say I'm overweight, and I do need to lose a few pounds by the way, and I told you that I just joined a gym and that my plan is to go to this gym and work out for twenty minutes a day, four days a week. ·en I told you my expectation is that I am going to get ripped abs within a month or two. Would you believe me when I told you I would be able to accomplish that outcome using that effort? Of course not. Even if you don't workout yourself, we all know that to get in amazing shape, it would take a lot more than simply one hour and twenty minutes a week and only a month or two. Especially if you started the process already overweight.

Most of us would instantly discount such a claim, whether we have ever gone to the gym, even for a day, or not. We all know that we cannot accomplish those types of results in so little time.

Well, the same is true for the forty-hour workweek. Let me tell you something clear as a bell. No one ever got rich by working forty hours a week. It is not possible, and whoever told you that, lied. No one who has taken business seriously would believe it; just as no bodybuilder or someone who used to be overweight but has ripped abs now would ever believe that someone could get those results in twenty minutes a day, four days a week. · ey would all fall off their chair laughing, because they know that no one has ever gotten ridiculously fit with ripped abs by working out for just twenty minutes a day, four times a week. It is simply not possible.

· e reality of it is that this forty-hour workweek has been a hoax perpetrated on you, the worker and business owner. It is a sad thing, and I am here to make sure that it never happens again. We are going to stop it, here and now and simply accept the fact that more time will always equal a greater result.

I have discovered, through twenty plus years of experience working with thousands of companies and individuals, that if you ever want to get good at making money, you have to dedicate a minimum—and definitely not a maximum—fifty hours per week. Typically, I always recommend fifty to fifty-five hours—consistently over an extended period of time, with a few weeks here and there—going sixty to seventy hours a week when you are trying to push for a big increase in revenue, skill set, and/or income goal.

If I just started a new job or a new project, I am going to dedicate sixty to seventy hours for a week or two to really make sure it is launched well. Once it is launched, I can dedicate a solid fifty to fifty-five hours a week to ensure it can grow and prosper and get me the results I want.

Fifty hours a week is the gold standard when it comes to a prosperous work-life balance. If you are not willing to hold yourself to those time standards, don't expect any major goal to be reached for your forty-hour work week it won't happen. What do those extra ten hours per week produce? Does it produce simply just another ten hours of watching the clock? Hopefully not. It is going to produce an extra week a month, an extra two months per year. · en that is significant.

If I'm working an extra ten hours a week, considering there are 4.3 weeks in a month, that is an extra forty-three hours a month, which is a whole extra week. If I get twelve weeks more over a year than anyone else, those are three extra months I get per year compared to anyone else who is only working forty hours per week. As you can realize I would have a tremendous competitive advantage over those people. I would outwork, outproduce, and outperform anyone else working just forty hours per week even if our skill set remained the same.

Also, with only forty hours a week, your skill set is not going to improve as fast as mine! If I am only working out twenty minutes a day at the gym, am I really getting any stimulus on my muscles? Am I really working up a sweat? Am I really getting my heart pumping? No. Anyone who has ever done anything physical for twenty minutes knows that after twenty minutes, you are just barely starting to get into it. You are barely beginning to operate at your peak performance level.

Well, it is the same way with forty hours in a workweek or eight hours in a workday. After eight hours, you are just barely starting to get up to your peak performance. It is not until you work the extra two hours a day that you really begin to dig into your true potential. In order to see gains in your skill sets, just like you want to see gains in your physique, you have got to push yourself further. If you don't push yourself far enough, you are not going to see any gains. · e only reason why your body or your mind has any reason to get better at anything is if it feels it needs it for survival. If you are never pushing yourself for those extra reps, or those extra hours, your brain will never be able to make the type of adjustments required to adapt to the new pressures and the new stimuli and hence will not get faster, bigger, better or stronger.

Remember that you still want to be results driven and not just time driven. · erefore, by no means does it produce more to go to the office and watch the clock for fifty hours. Just because you were there for fifty hours does not mean you are going to get better at something either. · at would be the same ridiculous conclusion as saying that you are going to go to the gym, and just because you were at the gym listening to music and watching people work out for two hours a day, you are now going to get ripped abs, a firm butt, and huge biceps. · at is not going to happen. You have to put in the work and effort while you put in the time. One without the other is simply a waste of the only thing that matters, TIME.

So, time means something or it means nothing. Time only becomes valuable if you are working hard. If you are not working hard, then time becomes valueless, simply hands on a clock. So, it's up to you to make your time the most valuable. Push for that $500 per hour value and hold yourself accountable.

Consistently working fifty to fifty-five hours a week, as long as you are working hard and for results will ensure that you are going to get better, stronger, and faster. Your skills will increase with the extra time as long as you are working your butt off while you are there, pushing the extra sets and the extra reps, and, above all, holding yourself completely accountable for getting it done and being results driven.

CHAPTER 12

Credit and Its Role in Success

So far, we have spoken a lot about what mentally goes into being successful and making money.

Starting in this chapter and moving forward with the rest of the book, we are going to really get into some practical, actionable financial strategies that will really propel you to being more successful.

We have discussed this a little in previous chapters but it really needs its own. ·e role credit plays in their overall success is a key foundation on which I always train my clients. Every part of the strategy is as important as the other, but this one really lays the foundation where every move you make on top of it would have a tremendously increased impact. It's a true magnifier.

If I can help you make another dollar, and you have good credit versus having bad credit, then that one extra dollar with good credit is the same as two extra dollars with bad credit. We have previously discussed how a $400-car payment does not always equal the same car. · erefore, understanding how proper credit is used and how to use the power of your good credit score is going to be something that you can really build on and is going to increase the value of not only your current money but also every dollar you make hereafter. Excellent credit and the ability to leverage money has unbelievable income-generating power.

So that said, let us talk about credit and why it is so valuable. Why do you need good credit? Why not just pay cash for everything? Well, let's break that down. Credit is important because when you have a really good credit score, you can leverage money at a rate that is low and that is extremely valuable to increase income.

With a good credit score, you can get car loans for as low as 3-4 percent, credit cards at 9-10 percent, personal loans at 6-7 percent, business loans in the 7–8 percent, and home loans in the 3–4.5 percent range. Basically, in the overall grand scheme of things, money that cheap is almost free. Typically, I tell my clients that anything below a 5-7 percent interest rate is almost like free money, and using cash instead of credit to buy something that is going to cost you an overall interest rate that low is foolish. · e value of cash on hand is worth way more than 6 percent, and I'll show you why later on in this book.

· us, if our credit score is very good, we can get really cheap money. In most cases, in my opinion, even what I like to call "free money,". · erefore, if we can get this next to "free money" then our strategy will be to keep our cash on hand, which will allow us to grow our business, take calculated risks and do things that we otherwise would not be able to do. It is always very important to stay somewhat cash-rich, and borrow money when it is beneficial to increasing your income or supporting the creation of more income. · is simple model can really propel you to increase your overall net worth and your income as well. Investing cash to buy down "good debt" is not a winning strategy, despite what your parents told you, and as any multimillionaire or billionaire will tell you.

Another thing to consider then is how to use credit properly. First, understand that if you saved a dollar in interest, that is another dollar that gets added to active income, which then can be added to your disposable income, and every dollar that you either didn't make or you needlessly threw away to a higher interest rate comes directly from your disposable income.

· e real power of disposable income is not savings as you have been told but instead as useable cash flow. Your basic living expenses are fixed, so basically you have your food, housing, vehicle expenses, health care, childcare, insurance, clothes, and entertainment. These things are fixed and should be tightly budgeted. These are what I call personal fixed costs or (PFCs).

When your costs are fixed, you only have a certain amount of predictable overhead that must be met every month. Every dollar of income that is greater than this overhead is another dollar that you can then use as disposable income for investments, which investments are smart? Not the ones you have been told but we'll get to later in the book. For now, understand that disposable income needs to be redeployed through investments to make more income, or if immediate income cannot be increased it can be saved to enhance your cash position such that you have greater maneuverability to make the most of the opportunities that may come your way that could increase your income. If I have cash on hand and there is a great opportunity to invest to open or grow my own business or buy something of high value that someone is willing to sale at wholesale prices, I can swoop in with the cash I have, buy it, invest in it, and flip it, thus making more income. Extra cash should always be first used to create more income!

If you don't have enough cash on hand or access to it, you are obviously going to be excluded from those kinds of opportunities. Therefore, it is imperative that you have a lot of cash on hand to deploy to create more income and never trade cash to pay off good debt at a low interest rate.

As you can see, your credit score is actually really valuable. I would say that good credit, valued for most professional working people, is worth about $300,000–$400,000 in real value and for high income earners and business owners it is worth millions of dollars. It is just as valuable as most people's houses and businesses, so don't take it for granted. When you have something as valuable as your house, you would obviously want to take care of it.

Therefore, let's talk about how to get good credit, because that is where the rubber is going to meet the road. Let us say you don't have good credit, or let us say you have marginal credit. How are you going to get good credit? Well, guess what? I have got some good answers.

Obviously, there are different types of starting credit that you could have. If you have no credit, meaning that you have never established credit lines, you would basically have a zero score. It is neither good nor bad; it simply means you have zero track record of credit. · ere is a certain score you would get just for having opened one line of credit with your name and a social security number, which is typically between 540 and 660 points depending on if that one line is good or bad. From there, it is going to either go up or down, depending on whether you have good or more bad payment history on your credit profile.

For example, let's assume that you simply have no credit. Since you don't have any credit, you cannot get a regular credit card. In this case, you would want to get two secured credit cards from any of the unlimited number of banks that offer them. · ey are easy to find. Basically, you want to look for the easy ones that are easily accepted, such as Visa or MasterCard.

I do recommend using Credit Karma to find the right one for you. I'm going to give Credit Karma a plug here. I think Credit Karma is great, and if you are not on it, you need to be! Now some banks will give you a $200 secured credit card with only $50 or $60 out of your pocket, and with others, you need to pay them a deposit of $200 to receive a $200 credit card. Either way, see if you can find some that will let you just pay the smaller fee, and then get a $200-$300 line of credit. Even if you have to put the whole amount into secure a secured credit card, do it. It is more than worth it.

· e funds will go into an interest-bearing bank account, so you don't lose the money you simply leverage your cash for the same amount of availability on the credit card. It is still your money and as long as you pay the credit card it will always be your money. It is just like putting it in a savings account. · e bottom line is that you will get a positive trade line on your credit report, and you are now going to build good credit off of it. · e credit bureaus will not know it is a secured credit card and it will report the same as an unsecured one.

· e trick with these cards is to not max them out, because then you are going to lower your credit score in some cases by 100 points. Instead, buy a little amount of gas on it, or maybe use it for a little trip to the grocery store. If you have a $200 secured credit card, you need to spend only $30-$40 bucks on it every month and immediately pay it off in full when you get the credit card statement. Do this with both cards, and you will see jumps in credit scores of up to 80–100 points within five to six months. It does depend on some other factors, but these will be huge jumps. You can go from a starting 600 score to a 700 score in a matter of a few months, not years.

Obviously, individual results will vary depending on other factors in your credit, but these are really tremendous ways to get major increases in credit scores without it costing a lot of money. It only takes a little amount of time and a few hundred dollars, and it can make a really big impact on your credit score.

Now, as soon as you have two small unsecured credit cards, and you get your score up to where other credit-card companies are looking to then give you unsecured credit cards, usually over 700, you'll want to go ahead and get two more of those unsecured credit cards for a total of four.

I found that two unsecured cards and two secured ones, bringing the number to four credit cards in total, with always carrying zero balances is going to maximize your score, and grant you a jump of 100-120 points typically off your starting score. Spend a little on them each month, get the points, and pay them off immediately before your credit report shows any balance due. If you are always showing a very low, if not zero, balance in all your credit cards, you'll maximize your score very quickly.

Having more than four or five cards like that will impact your score the other way, so four and no more than five credit cards is optimum.

ese are quick, legitimate, easy, and fast ways to really increase your credit score, which would then open up the opportunity for you to leverage money cheap and easy for car loans, business loans and home loans.

With a high score you can go to any car dealership in this country, walk on the lot, and put zero money down on any vehicle you like and drive it off. It is a sign-and-drive situation in most cases. Because my credit score is always in the 780–800 range, I can buy any brand-new car at 0–3 percent interest with no money down. Some of these car dealers or manufacturers will even give you 0 percent interest with good credit even on seventy-two-month financing. · at is not only free money but you could literally be getting paid for that money through the increased value of the use of the new vehicle in your business or job.

Good credit also matters when you apply for a job and someone pulls up your credit score as part of the interview process or the background check, and, all of a sudden, your credit score comes up at 750–780. Now the recruiter goes, "Oh, wow, look at this! We have a very responsible person." · is is how doors open and high-level hiring is conducted in a lot of companies.

Beyond just the money, savings, buying ability, and the fact that you can get a really nice car for $400 versus a piece of junk for $400, understand that anyone who pulls your credit for whatever reason, whether it is a job opportunity, business deal or maybe if you are moving into an apartment building, they all look at your credit score. If you have a knockout credit score, it is going to get you better deals faster, and it is going to get you preferential treatment over others with lesser scores. · erefore, you have to have good credit at all costs. After all, to the average professional it is worth about $400,000 or more so make it happen.

Now, as I mentioned in the previous chapter, we were discussing how to settle bad debt. I do have tons of videos on YouTube about this, but I am going to cover it here, and then I will refer you to my YouTube videos and online course for the greater specifics.

So let us say you pull your credit score, and there is some medical bill you did not pay, or you moved out of some apartment, and there were damages the deposit didn't cover or extra unpaid rent that was still due on the lease, or there were some library books you did not return, or you had a credit-card bill you did not pay. ·ese things happen to a lot of good people. You are not alone. So, now what? Each of these would lower your credit score, and it could sit there for a period of seven years, digging into and lowering your credit score. So clearly as you now know the power of good credit you need to get it settled out! If you have bills, you have to pay them. Not paying your bills is not an option.

·is is a far too common example that I have helped many people with. Say you lived in an apartment when you were younger. You broke the lease, you owe $3,000, and it is sitting on your credit report as reported by the creditor or a collection agency. ·e first thing you need to do is contact the creditor or collection agency and ask them who the creditor currently is. ·ey will tell you whether it is still the apartment building, or if the debt has been sold off to somebody else. Now, if the debt has been sold off, that should give you some opportunity to get a better settlement, because they paid less for it. If, however, it has not been sold off, and it is still with the original creditor, you are not going to be able to get as good a deal to settle but I'll still teach you how to get a great settlement deal.

Now, the key to getting a good deal is to never call them and tell them that you have a ton of money, and you want to settle it up, because then they are going to want the whole thing, plus interest and costs. However, you want to tell them the truth, right? So do so and tell them that you are still a little down on your luck. You are still struggling. You would like to get this taken care of because it has been weighing on you. You just do not feel right owing people money, and you want to try to settle it. You have a relative, or a friend, who can lend you some money if the deal is right, but this person is only going to lend you the money if the debt is removed from your credit, not just updated or marked that is paid or settled. Make that clear up front, and get it in writing. Now, especially if it is an older debt, they are more than likely going to be fine with that.

From there, start at 30 percent on the dollar. · ey will typically jump at that. At most, you might have to go up to 50–60 percent on the dollar, but you can usually get settlements somewhere close to 30-50 percent. Now, I cannot give you any guarantees. Some people are harder than others, and some are not going to give you any kind of settlement at all, but at least you can still ask. So, $3,000 worth of bad debt could get settled for $1500 and get removed from your credit. Again, remember what your credit is worth $400,000, and so you are absolutely going to want to pay $1,500 to get a good credit score back. As soon as the bad stuff is removed, or even at the same time you can get the two secured credit cards, and as soon as your credit is about 700, you can start getting unsecured credit cards. With any bad debt now settled and removed and only good credit being reported you can pump your credit score up to 720-750 really quick. Once you are there you are now in the driver's seat, and you can get whatever you want, whenever you want on credit at a great rate. · at is really a powerful and lucrative position to be in.

Now, the next thing to do, once you do get good credit, if you do have anything like a car loan or a house loan to which you are currently paying a higher interest rate, you can go ahead and refinance those to lower rates and save yourself a lot more money on those rates.

For instance, if you have a house at 5-6 percent, because your credit was a little iffy, or you have a FHA loan, now that you have great credit, you can go conventional and get your interest rate lowered down to the 3.5–4 percent range and save a lot of money there. Remember a dollar you save on interest is better than a dollar earned, because it is a dollar that can directly go into your disposable income and be used to then create even more income. Now that is the power of leverage.

CHAPTER 13

When and What to Invest In

Now, I get this question a lot. Obviously, everybody wants to know what to invest in. "Cory, where should I put my money? Cory, I got twenty bucks; where should it go? Cory, I got $1,000; what should I do with it? Cory, I got $10,000; what should I do with it? Cory, I got $50,000; what should I do with it?"

My answer is always the same, and it goes like this: "· e first thing that you are always going to invest in, no matter what, is yourself."

Now, I know that is a little confusing. What does that mean to invest in yourself? Well, the first thing you have to realize is that you are your own best asset. So, when I say invest in yourself first, here is what I'm talking about.

No initial consumer investment in the world is going to have the ability to make more money than you do through direct income. · ings like stocks, bonds, and real estate, none of it has the income potential that you have as your own business venture. So, what should you invest in? Yourself. Unless your income is actually maxed out—and I am not even sure what that is, but maybe for the sake of being practical if you are making $500,000 to 1 million a year, you would have come close to maxing out your direct income potential depending on your individual career and chosen vehicle. · is does not include if you are a business owner and have employees or the ability to scale your business enterprise. If that is the case then you can never max out your potential. · is is to be used as an example of you simply working as a high-level executive, licensed professional or a top tier salesperson. Can you make a million a year driving a van by yourself? Probably not. Can you do so if you went from being a van driver to the top salesperson working for a company that owned a fleet of vans and hired drivers? Absolutely! So, once you are at the $500,000 to one-million-a-year mark, then you can start making investments in commercial property, multi-family real estate, other business ventures, and so forth. But until you are making $500,000 to one million a year, the only thing you should invest in is you! Nothing else is going to give you a bigger, recession proof and more controllable return on investment period.

Still doubt me? Let's do the math. A typical return of investment that is considered very favorable—as most financial managers would tell you—is around 7-8 percent for a stock portfolio, 7-10 percent for real estate investment, and 20–25 percent if you invested in an individual private business venture, all of these are highly risky by the way. If you can even meet these return numbers, you are doing very well, and it would be exceptional. As you can see, the percentages of return on normal boilerplate investments are not really that high. Yes, they can compound over the years, and you can certainly save your way to a little bit of money after thirty to forty years of doing this, but should you? I challenge you to do the math on what I call "PSI" (Personal Self-Investment). And a simple rule I like to call the 50/5 rule. Let's compare PSI to typical investments like stocks or real estate. For instance, if you invested in PSI instead of either saving money or regular boilerplate investments, how much new income can you create? · ink of this, if you could add at least a 50 percent increase in year-over-year income every single year for five years in a row, how much would that be? I bet if you took your current income and increased it by 50 percent every year for five years, that increase would easily trounce any amount of compounding return at 7-8 percent that you would get if you put that same money in the stock market. Yes? Yes! Let's take a look at what the 50/5 rule can do. What is the 50/5 rule? It's simply taking your current income and increasing it by 50 percent every year for five years. For instance, the average income that the US Census Bureau shows for the average American worker is only $59,000 per year. For now, let's focus on the how then I'll show you the numbers of the 5/50 rule even starting at that average income as an example of the power of PSI combined with the 50/5 rule.

So how much should you invest in yourself to get this amazing 50% return? Well, this is a little more complicated, but a solid budget can be set. First, you need to invest enough to increase your skills and then your income by 50 percent and then do the work based upon your new skills. ·e investment will consist of time, then money to achieve education via books, training courses, seminars, and classes to acquire new skills and new strategies that will help you achieve the new skills and hence the 50% increase. I have personally spent tens of thousands of dollars on training courses, personal-enhancement courses, and online courses over my career. I have attended seminars and read more books than I can count, and I still do so to this day! Why? It's the constant education that allows me to grow my income year over year. You cannot do the same thing you did last year and expect your income to increase this year. In addition to paying for books, courses, and seminars, make sure that you are also using YouTube as much as possible. In addition to the paid stuff, and as I previously mentioned, there is also a ton of free resources that have tons of value as well including YouTube. You cannot miss it. Anything and everything you want to know is on YouTube and taught by many different voices. Never discount the value in hearing the same ideas from different people. ·ere is no such thing as one source for any information. Every teacher, coach, guru, and mentor has a different perspective, so reach out for as many as you can that make sense to you. Sometimes hearing how someone did it wrong is also very valuable. Knowing what mistakes not to make is also an extremely valuable education and don't discount it.

In addition to the freebies out there on YouTube, use Google to find and take paid online courses from credible people who are relevant to who you are and what you are trying to accomplish. Anything that teaches you how to manage money, or increase your income and your skills is highly valuable. If you are a real estate agent, as an example, take courses on not just how to sell real estate but also on how to market real estate, find it, fix it, flip it, and know the laws that control it. · e more you know overall about real estate, the better of an agent you are going to be. So why should you still pay for coaching when it's free on other platforms? Because no expert is going to give you his or her best information for free! · e free stuff will give you a solid understanding of the subject matter, but the real professional ins and outs will be missed. Again, you need to spend money on your education so you get the best education you can. Do you think Harvard costs the same as a local community college? Of course not, and you know why. Quality education costs money, and you need to spend some to get it. So, don't cheap it out. Be smart. Don't fall for every self-proclaimed guru on the planet, but seek out truly qualified coaches that resonate with you, and if their free stuff makes sense to you, don't be afraid to sign up for the paid stuff; it will be worth its weight in gold I assure you.

Additionally, also take courses on how to do things apart from just increasing your income, such as courses on how to grow a business, how to start a business, how to create extra income streams within your job or business, accounting, legal issues, and so forth. · ere is a lot of training to be done and a lot of knowledge to be acquired if you want to maximize your income and wealth. · ere is no skipping it, and if your goal is to increase your income year after year, you definitely have to do it. Overall, you would want to create a budget for your continuing education. · ink of it as going to a university every year and getting a new degree every year. I typically spend anywhere between $10,000–$30,000 a year on continuing education. I have come a long way, and I have a long way to go, but I would say that anything in that range is going to allow you to acquire the results you seek to continue to grow your income at the rate described above. · e 50/5 rule is very achievable and I personally did it! But it takes constantly acquiring new skills and new strategies and you must make a commitment to get the work done and grow.

No, I did not forget that I promised you the math on the 50/5 percent increase in income above but I wanted you to understand the investment part first. So now that we understand the value of our continuing education and what to invest and expect, let's calculate our ROI (Return on Investment) of doing so. Let's say, for example, you are beginning at an income of the $59,000 per year. Using my 50/5 rule, you should look to increase your income by 50 percent of that starting figure for five years in a row. Below are the years starting with the base year and the increases per year and the result at the end of a five-year period.

Base Year: $59,000 Year 1: $88,500, Year 2: $135,750, Year 3: $199,125, Year 4: $298,687, Year 5: $448,030. · at's (8X) your base year income in only five years. You can also keep going and do my 10/5 rule as well. By year 10 you'd be at a whopping $2,268,150!

As you can see, by using my 50/5 rule you should be making up to or near $500,000 per year by the fifth year, which is actually more than eight times your starting pay. · at's an—800 percent—increase or ROI in only 5 years.

Now let's apply it to someone making $40,000 per year. If they go from $40,000 to $60,000 in the first year and spent $5,000 on training and education in the first year, that is a $20,000 first-year return on their $5,000 investment. · at is a 400 percent return on investment (ROI). You see why this hands down beats conventional boilerplate investing? · is proves that investing in yourself first is always the way to go, and no other investments you can make will even come close to making that kind of return on your investment money. · e other major benefit of investing in yourself is that it's as safe of an investment as you can make. No other safe and riskless investment has that kind of ROI potential. I'm sure now you see why it's so important to keep investing in yourself through a minimum of the Five-Year Plan. If you take it to Ten years then the math on ROI is almost scary to even calculate. Am I getting through to you yet?

After you reach your five-year income goal, you can now, if you wish, invest in normal boilerplate investments like stocks, bonds, and real estate. However, never look for a hustle or a little gimmick investment. I see a lot of high-income people lose money trying to swing for home runs after they make a good income. Flipping real estate is one well-known way to lose money. Remember 2008? True, it is not that people don't make money that way, but it is not something you should be trying to do if you are making $40,000–$50,000 a year! Nor should you do it if you need to use your entire cash savings. Once you start making $400,000–$500,000 a year, and you want to invest $50,000, go for it. If you lose the fifty grand, it does not matter. But if you are making forty grand a year, and you lose a whole year's worth of income in some kind of side-hustle get-rich-quick scheme, it is going to leave a mark. Invest in yourself first and not until your income is at much higher levels do you ever consider any other kind of investment. As you now know it just does not make any sense.

CHAPTER 14

Should You Own Your Own Business or Stay Employed?

My understanding after coaching businesses for twenty years is that not everybody is meant to be in business. It is just a simple fact. Not everybody is cut out to be in business, nor should most even try to be in business. · e reality of it is that sometimes employment is the better solution, depending on the lifestyle you want and the level of risk you can tolerate. For some, being a W2 employee for the entirety of their career is just right. For others, the entrepreneurial bug bites them, and they must simply be their own boss. However, very often, I see that people in W2 positions make more money than their business-owner counterparts. · ere are many factors that go into whether you will make more money as a W2 or as a business owner, and there are certainly a lot of sacrifices to be made choosing either. Before you decide whether employment or owning a business is right for you or whether you would like to start your own business, consider the following number of variables that will help you make a better decision.

Since most of you are probably curious about what owning your own business entails, let me tell you the benefits and then the drawbacks of owning a business. I have owned several businesses over the period of nearly two decades, and I am pretty familiar, I'd even say an expert, regarding all the benefits and the drawbacks. Knowing both is very important because that would have to be a major part of your decision-making process. You cannot make your decisions in life based upon only the benefits. You have to also weigh the negatives, the consequences, and the sacrifices. For every decision you make, there are always going to be negatives that go along with it, and there are certainly going to be things that you would rather not do. For business owners those decisions are what I call business sacrifices. Being in business entails a number of large sacrifices, most of which people do not want to make. ·e sad reality is that people who don't face the facts upfront concerning the sacrifices business owners must make to be successful are usually in for a rude awakening. Most businesses and business owners who fail, do so because of the simple reason that they did not calculate the sacrifices that were going to be necessary to become a successful business owner. When I advise a business owner of the whys and why-nots of being in business, the first thing I tell them is that it is not about the risks and the rewards; it is about the sacrifices. If you don't make the proper sacrifices, you can forget about receiving any rewards, and you would certainly experience and receive all the negatives.

·at said, there are a number of basic rules I have for anyone in business or even thinking of getting into business, and they are as follows:

·e first question I ask anyone who is in or wants to get into business is, "How much money do you make now not being in business?" And I'm typically not surprised by the answers. ·e reality of it is that most people who tell me they would like to be in business simply don't make very much money at their current jobs. ·ey dream of being in business for the sole purpose of the riches and rewards that they think will simply present themselves. ·e fantasy always is there will be a life of luxury, with a flexible schedule, where they can be washing their Mercedes in the driveway at two o'clock on a Wednesday afternoon. ·e reality of it is that nothing can be farther from the truth.

Let me tell you firsthand, not only from running multiple businesses over two decades but also working with literally thousands of business owners, that there is no such thing as a glamorous business owner lifestyle, especially initially. ·e glamor lifestyle is a fantasy made up by those who would trick you into believing that being in business is some easy path to riches and glory and comfort all while working just twenty hours a week. Let me make it clear it is simply not that at all. As a matter of fact, being in business is a much bigger sacrifice than being employed.

Is it flexible? Sure. Do you have to work every day? No. But the second you are not working every day, let me tell you, your business will suffer. So, you can either take time off and watch your business suffer and fail, or you can saddle up for seven days a week and make it prosper.

· erefore, the first test you are going to have to pass if you want to hope to be profitable in business is the sacrifice test. And most people are not ready for the sacrifice and fail this test. ·is unwillingness to sacrifice is why a vast majority of businesses fail within the first five years; not because they did not have great ideas and products, or because the owners were not smart enough or intelligent enough, or did not have enough experience, but because they simply did not calculate the sacrifices that were going to be necessary to make the business successful. · erefore, they end up underworking, and within two to five years or less, they fail.

Do you want to start or stay in business? · en answer should be based on this. Are you really prepared to do whatever it takes? Now, a lot of people confuse whatever it takes with what they would like it to take. Just like anyone else on the face of this planet, I want things to be easier. I want the easy button. Who doesn't? You would be a fool not to desire those things. But let me tell you, here and now, unequivocally, they do not exist. If you believe there is a shortcut in business and that you can do what you want and hope that it takes less, let me assure you right here and right now, it is going to take twice of whatever you can imagine in the best-case scenario. · at will help wrap your brain around what it really takes to get into business and or to own a successful business.

In the truest sense, whatever it takes literally means whatever it takes. When I started my first business in the year 2000, the first thing that I decided to do was to lay out my schedule for the first three months of the businesses start date. Now, having some knowledge and having managed several businesses up to this point, albeit not being the owner but being a senior manager in charge, I had a clear understanding of what it would really take to be successful. · e first schedule I laid out for myself consisted of seven days a week, twelve hours a day. · erefore, for the first few months in business, I decided my schedule would be from 7:00 a.m. to 7:00 p.m., seven days a week: I call it the 7-7-7 or "Blackjack" rule. · is is an easy thing to remember and understand. If you want to be successful in starting a business, apply the Blackjack rule first and foremost. Do that for the first three months. If it is still not working, and if your business is still not hitting your planned goals then you need to increase the hours. You may have to work from 5:00 a.m. to 10:00 p.m. Now, I do believe in giving yourself enough time for some sleep, but that is it: Sleep, shower and work. Why didn't I mention eating? Because you can do that on your way to and from work. ·· is structure is the real "whatever it takes". If you have to literally work fifteen hours a day, seven days a week, to make your business work, you better be prepared to do it and with a smile on your face. If you are not fully prepared to do that, let me tell you this right now: do not get into business, because oftentimes that is what it takes.

Now, thankfully for me, my 7-7-7 Blackjack rule worked out perfectly. I went 7:00 a.m. to 7:00 p.m., seven days a week for the first three months. By the second month, we were in the black. By the third month, we were extremely profitable, and I never looked back. · e reality of it is that I went in correctly. Can you do the same? Can you put in the time? Will you make the sacrifice with regard to the time? If the answer is no, do not get into business period stay as a W2 or contract worker.

Now, this is the second test I give people. Do you make at least $10,000 a month, or at least $100,000 a year, in your W2 or contract job? If you do not make at least $100,000 a year in your job, I highly doubt you have the skills yet necessary to really bring a truly valuable service or product to the market. If you have not proven your value to the owner of the company you work for enough for them to be willing to pay you $100,000 a year, or if you have failed to ask and sell yourself to them to get the $100,000 a year, that tells me that you do not have the skills required to be in business yet.

Let me explain further. Is it true that most business owners are not going to come up to you and offer you $100,000 a year to do sales, manage or run their business? Of course, there are. But if you never stopped to negotiate a better deal with the boss to get those opportunities then how do you think you'll have the skills to negotiate tough business deals? If your skills are not there yet then do not start a business. Instead work on your skills first to get at least to there then you can start the business.

· erefore, let me give you the exact way you should approach your boss to get that type of position and pay structure first and it goes exactly like this, "Hey, Boss I want to make at least $100,000 a year. Give me the list of things I need to do to be worth that to you?" Now only two things will happen. Either the boss will give you the list and you prove to them you can do it and then negotiate the contract to make the $100K a year or the boss will say there is no list. Now if the boss says there is no list it's time to move on to a new company. When you apply for the new job in the interview make it clear what your income goals are and then ask the same question of them. Not until someone gives you the list that will allow you to make $100,000 in their organization do you take the job. I guarantee you by the second or third interview they are going to hirer you just because you asked that question. Now if you can't do these little things to get your first $100,000 job then I don't think you are going to be equipped to own and run a business successfully. Let me tell you before you make the mistake of doing so, the biggest skill you are going to need if you want to consider opening up a business is excellent Sales skills. If you cannot sell your boss on paying you what you are worth and provide that level of value to them, how are you going to sell effectively to customers? If you can't provide that kind of value to your boss how are you going to provide that level of value to customers? Let me give you a shocking insight. All of us are already both business owners as well as employees! Even business owners have a boss and they are called customers. And even as an employee you really need to think, conduct yourself and operate as a business. ·e requirements are the same both ways trust me and doing so will help you to maximize income.

So those are the two key tests I always have for anyone. First, are you really willing to put in the sacrifice? Are you willing to play Blackjack and do a 7-7-7 schedule for the first several months? If you are not willing to then forget about it. Second, do you make $100,000 a year in your current position, or in a past position, where you were running a business, managing a sales department, being a top salesperson, or being a top producer? If the answer is no, then, again, I don't think you have the skills yet to be in business. Chances are that you are going to fail miserably and make less money than you did at your job and run through your life savings.

So, where does that leave you in this decision? It depends on how you answered the two questions? If you answered yes to both and you have the money saved up to pay for startup costs and six months of operating and personal expenditures then go for it! If you answered no to either question then it leaves you needing more skill set and personal development work to be done. Refer to the previous chapters of this book to learn how to do both and get to work!

Now, let us say that you are ready to start a business because you answered yes to all the questions. Let us say that you are willing to work from 7:00 a.m. to 7:00 p.m., seven days a week. Let us suppose that you have made or do make $100,000 a year in your current position and have the cash on hand to start the business. Good. Now, let us talk about the benefits of owning your own business. Of course, the biggest benefit I have ever perceived in running a business is not the fantasy stuff. ·ere is no freedom in running a business.

Businesses are 24-7 propositions and 365 days a year. You are going to find yourself on Christmas preparing for year-end, checking emails, bank accounts, and financials, licensing, insurance, and everything else. It goes on and on and on. ·e list is too extensive. You will never have a day off, so get that out of your head. Owning a successful business is not about the fantasy freedom. ·en what is it about? What are the benefits of running your own business? ·e number one thing that I tell everyone who wants to own their own business is that the only reason you should ever want to own a business is because you want to control your own destiny. ·at is the only true benefit. You get to follow your own vision not someone else's. And yes, if you do it very well you will make more money because you are able to directly help a lot more people with the biggest problem that you know how to solve.

·e reason why I got into business for myself twenty years ago was because I felt the need to control my own destiny. I had been working for other organizations for about seven years and I was making a strong six-figure income. I managed teams of people for several years and always produced high returns in whatever position I was engaged in. So, from the standpoint of a skill set, I was absolutely ready. I was also already in a position of being able to work seven days a week, 7:00 a.m. to 7:00 p.m. But the big key that made it worthwhile for me was the prospect of being able to control my own destiny. I had gotten sick and tired of the glass ceiling. I wanted more. I wanted to see how far I could really go. I wanted the personal challenge of knowing, "Hey, how good can I really be? How much value can I really bring to the marketplace if I'm in charge? And how many people in my organization, employees, and other people whom I touch can I help? How many clients can I help? What kind of value could I bring to my customers and my clients if I was the owner?"

·ese were the biggest driving forces for me, and I can tell you right now that for any business owner who ever becomes very successful at it, those have to be your main motivating factors. You have to want to control your own destiny to see just how far you can go, and you want to be able to provide as much value for your employees and your customers as possible. ·ose are always the two best driving forces for any successful business owner.

Another solid benefit is to be able to pick the people you work with. As a business owner, you get the ability to decide who you work with and who you work for. ·at is another empowering thing that makes it really worthwhile to be in business. Obviously, you can also dictate where your business goes, what markets it goes in, and who it affects. You can decide to take on new tasks and new challenges, branch out, maybe expand, or you can decide to keep it in the spare bedroom of your house. You decide. ·at really is the best benefit of running your own business. But, in my case, I wanted a real challenge. I wanted to be able to challenge myself to see how far I could go. But that has to be a decision every business owner makes for themselves. ·e only thing I say is required is that you must grow it at least to get up to that magical $500,000 per year profit so you can help those that you are obligated to as previously mentioned. After that if you are fine there then stay there and ride it out. If you want more then go get it! If you grow then you will end up having the pride that comes from only something that you built yourself and you can stand back and say, "Look at that. I built that." I can tell you, that is a fantastic feeling.

If you check all these boxes, if you are willing to make the sacrifices and willing to step up and get it done, then I encourage you to get into business, if that is your passion. If not then be content in your contract employ and simply get the skills and information needed to get to that $500,000 per year mark. Nothing wrong with that whatsoever.

·erefore, if there is a true upside to being employed then let us talk about the benefits and also the drawbacks of being employed. To be clear there are also major sacrifices in being an employee. ·e number one sacrifice is that you are always going to be at the will of someone else. If the boss or the owner wants something done, whether you agree with it or not, you have to do it. To me, that was always the biggest sacrifice in being employed. Now, did I have my say? Did I give my input into what was going to happen? Slightly. ·at is all it is ever going to be. You may have some influence in your organization, but at the end of the day, you have to be fully prepared to implement the boss's or owner's desires. If they want it a certain way, you are going to have to do it.

As an employee, I always made this promise to anybody who I ever worked for: "Now, I may not agree with you claiming that standing on my head in my chair for twelve hours a day is the right thing to do, but if you tell me that is what you want, I would get it done." If you are going to be an employee, understand you are not in control, and whatever is required of you, you have to get it done, as long as it is ethical, legal and moral of-course.

I would say that not being able to control your own schedule would be a negative of being employed, but truly, that is not the case. All my employees take much more time off than I ever do. · ey get that luxury. · ey are a cog in a wheel, whereas I am the axle. If I'm not there, the wheel cannot function. If they are on leave, the wheel will continue to spin and move the machine. · at is actually a benefit.

What are some of the other benefits? Of course, not having all the responsibility is a benefit. If something ultimately does not work or goes wrong, it is usually not on you. It is on some other employee or on the owner of the company for not making a good decision. Not having that responsibility is a big weight off your shoulders. When I was employed, I witnessed many mistakes being made, but I knew that they were not my mistakes, and I slept well at night knowing that I was still doing a great job. · at is a big benefit.

Another benefit to being employed is that you often have benefits paid for or subsidized like insurance and retirement plans. You might have a great insurance package for your family through your employer. Let me tell you, being self-employed, you have to pay for all that, and it is a lot of money these days, as we all know.

Another benefit of being an employee is the ability to change jobs within the organization, and also the ability to switch organizations. I worked for five different companies doing what I do before I opened my own business. Each one offered me a greater opportunity, more flexibility, more money, and more input, so I moved around a bit. I was really known as a hired gun. Once companies learned of my skill set, I was recruited heavily. By the end of my employment days a number of competitors in the industry were all competing over my services and that was a great position to be in. · erefore, I was always getting a phone call asking me to come to work for somebody, and four times, I decided that was a good idea. As a contract employee changing your income vehicle is not only necessary but very smart. If you hit the income ceiling at any company you work or contract for you must not sit there you must switch so that you can make sure you continue the 50/5 rule of income growth. Never let a limiting vehicle slow you down.

So those are the major benefits of being employed. For a lot of them you don't have that kind of flexibility if you own your own business. If you are the owner of your own business, that is it. You are there. · at is the company. · at is it. Now, can you change some things? Of course, you can, but it is like turning the Titanic. It is not as easy as turning a little speedboat when you are self-employed; you can do 180 degrees anytime you like. Owning a business, you have to be sure that you are able to navigate the rough seas and still keep the ship afloat. Also, I would definitely not recommend that you name your company the Titanic or anything to do with Failure. In my years of consulting I have seen both names used to my amazement. Needless to say, they all failed. Lesson? Yes, never be too cute or overly witty with your branding trust me. More of that in the next book so stay tuned.

If you're employed now and still want to open your own business in the future, but you just aren't ready to make the sacrifices right now or you are not making the $10,000 a month or $100,000 a year that is required. Well, no problem. I was there too. Again, I worked for seven years for other companies before I ever decided to open my own. And, in several of those companies, I was making strong six figures and working seven days a week, so I already understood the sacrifice and the skill set. If you are not there yet, here is what I suggest. Take your current situation at your current job, and maximize it by following the 50/5 rule. Obviously, the premise of this book is to maximize your now regardless if you are an employee or a business owner. ·e first step, if you ever want to become a business owner, is to maximize the sacrifices you are currently making as well as maximize your income right now at your job.

·erefore, start working more hours, at least fifty to fifty-five hours a week, as we have discussed, and possibly more, if you can. And, secondly, get your income up to over six figures as soon as possible. Now, if you are already providing a six-figure value to your employer, then the problem is that you have not sold yourself to your employer, and you need to learn how to do that immediately. A key part of making more money is not only providing a high value but also recognizing you are providing a high value and knowing how to go to the boss to sell yourself to be able to get the bigger salaries and bigger bonuses.

Again, as we discussed in the previous part of this chapter and other chapters, it is not going to be about asking your boss to just pay you more. You have to go to your boss and say, "I want to make six figures here. Give me the list of things I need to achieve to have you pay me six figures." · en, if the boss won't give you that list, it may be time to move on to somewhere else that will. If the boss does give you that list, which most absolutely will, then start working on it immediately. Even if you don't make the six figures right away, your income is still going to increase, and so is your skill set and your understanding of real sacrifice, because that boss is probably going to give you a pretty heavy list to get to six figures. Well, if you are going to get in business for yourself, you better learn how to do those things right now anyway. If you can't do it at your comfy job when you are employed, you certainly are not going to be able to do it when you are self-employed. Do not get into business until you understand how to make at least six figures in a job, which includes how to provide a six-figure value, and how to get your boss to pay you six figures. · ese are two skills that you are going to need if you ever hope to stay in business successfully.

· ink skills and customers. Your boss, in a way, is still your customer, and the skills you are providing still have value. Again, think of yourself as a business even when you are still and employee.

Any fool can get in business. Only the ones who check the above boxes can stay in business long term and make good money. Until you have the skills, and you are ready to make the sacrifices, don't get into business. Stay employed until you are ready. Work on those skills now, day and night. Educate, train, learn, employ, and channel your skill set, your ability, and your sacrifices at your job. You are going to make more money now, which can be life changing money as well. See how far you can go, right here, right now at your job. · at is going to be the first hurdle you need to cross. · ere are many W2 employees who make millions of dollars per year, so it's not a matter of limiting income. It's a matter of the willingness to sacrifice, gain skill sets that have high value and holding yourself accountable to getting it done. After that there really is no limit with whichever you choose. · e limit will always be your skill set, chosen organization and your efforts. Whether you stay W2 or go into business, once you have given yourself the education, training, and skills that will help you get a 50 percent increase in income year over year during the five-year period of the 50/5 rule, you will be in full control of your income from now on. · en it's on to the 50/10 rule hell ya!

What if you already own a business that is not doing well enough for you to make $500,000 per year? No, I didn't forget you either so let's dive in there next on exactly what to do immediately so you can save yourself. First, unless your business already makes you over $500,000 a year in profit, which is probably not the case, then you have no business in investing in anything but the growth of that business. Every part of this book pertains to your business the same as if it was its own person because it is. You must follow the same rules I have laid out just the same whether you are a business or person who is not making $500,000. Simply follow the same rules and they will work. Remember we are all businesses and we are all employees. Many business owners, especially ones that struggle, fail to invest in their own businesses but instead take the profit out and either live too high a lifestyle or invest in underperforming outside investments. As we discussed in previous chapters, the highest returns on investments you can ever achieve is in yourself and your own business. So even if your business is underperforming right now you need to follow these rules.

· e same would also apply if you are in a career that truly has an unlimited amount of income-earning potential, think-licensed professionals—that is, architects, dentists, lawyers, doctors, or other sales-based professions. If you own your own business already or if you are a licensed professional or sales professional, all you are going to continue to do is take the extra disposable income that you make, and you are going to put it back into the business or your professional position until you make at least $500,000 per year. You are not going to invest in things like IRAs and 401Ks unless you are trapped as a W2 employee somewhere where you cannot control your income as quickly or where your employer would match your contributions. Perhaps you are in government work or the medical profession. If you are in that situation and your boss refuses to give you the opportunity to make $500,000 a year then either find an employer that will or go start your own business. So, if you are going to trap yourself in a W2 situation like that, make sure it is in something where you can grow your income level as well as take advantage of the employer-provided benefits. Even if you are a nurse and you can only make a certain amount of income, but if you go back and get your master's degree, you can become a nurse practitioner to improve your licensure and hence increase your income.

· ere are a lot of ways, even if you are in a W2 position, for you to reinvest in your higher education and better skillsets to continue to grow your income. · ere is really not a point where you have maximized your income below $500,000 regardless of your chosen profession. · ere is always away to increase income and until you can maximize your income, there is truly no point to invest money on outside investments unless or until it is not impeding the growth of your income. So if you are sufficiently investing in yourself, and your income is growing by 50 percent, and you still have extra money left over—which you should—then yes, you would be looking for some more traditional boilerplate investments to do some savings increase your cash reserves, but not until then; until then just grow your income!

CHAPTER 15

What Exactly Is Sales? And Why Does Everyone Need to Be Great at It?

·roughout most of this book, you have heard me reference skill set. Your skills are the accumulation of the tools, knowhow and abilities you have available to you to complete tasks. Now, there are a number of skills one can have, from computer skills, writing skills, professional skills, various trade skills, math skills, customer service skills, building skills, drawing skills, and so forth. However, the one shining skill that everyone must have and most do not, especially if they ever want to make great money, is sales skills.

Sales skills are paramount. Sales is the skill for which all other skills are actually acquired and used. ·e skills that you employ at your work exist because somebody is selling something to somebody. Without the sale occurring first, what would your skills be used on? What customer would you be providing your customer-service skills to? Whatever skills you have, if there was never a sale to a customer, how could it ever be applied to the business? Most people think that customers magically appear. ·ey don't. Someone in your organization is driving sales and if they are not that organization is in deep trouble.

Therefore, the number one most valuable skill that can be acquired by everyone is sales skills, because without them, no other skills will be needed. Why then are there not many people with really good sales skills? One reason is most people believe they are afraid of doing sales and therefore never decided to get great at it. However, I can tell you, from the time we are five years old, we are some of the greatest salespeople who ever walked the face of the Earth. Some of the greatest salespeople whom I have ever seen in my career are four- and five-year-old children in a store, selling their parents on why they should get the toy or the piece of candy they desire.

If you ever want to see great salespeople at work, simply go down to your local department store, go to the toy section, and watch the kids start selling to their parents. They are ruthless. They have the greatest sales skills the game has ever seen. They can close, they can overcome all objections, they are relentless in their ability to persuade, coerce, and convince their parents to get them what they want. All the sales skills you would require are on full display in the pitch of a five-year-old to a parent over getting something they desire. A five-year-old kid knows every single one of the best sales techniques and exactly when to use them. Where exactly did these amazing abilities come from? We all have them built in. We just need to be reminded of that and tap back into them. Let's examine the techniques a five-year old would use as we all have inside us.

The child always starts the sale the same way: "Mom, Dad, I want this toy. I want this piece of candy." They make no qualms about it. What they want is stated upfront and with clear conviction. They tell the parent, "This is what I want." There is no hesitation, no holding back, and no apology. The parent knows exactly what the child wants, and the child has made it clear.

This is the first rule of sales. Always make your intentions absolutely clear as a bell upfront and without apology. Never try to disguise what you are after. There is no shame in it. As a matter of fact, you should wear it as a badge of honor. You should put it out there front and center. "I want this, and I make no apologies." If you can accept that and get over your fear of doing so, you are already halfway to being a good salesperson.

Now, before we get into actual skills more, let's first talk about why you want to be good at sales. I mean do you really need it? Yes! And there are a lot of reasons, some of which I have already mentioned in this and previous chapters but let's refresh because I really can't state it enough, you need great sales skills!

· e first and biggest incentive should be the simple fact that the highest paying jobs in almost any organization are always going to be the sales jobs. · e head of the sales department and the senior salespeople are the ones who really drive production. · ese are the people who are making the big money in most organizations. · ey are typically right behind the CEO, the CFO, and other higher-ranking officers of any organization on pay scale. In fact, in medium and small businesses, the top salespeople usually make even more money than the business owner does.

Imagine that. If you are a great salesperson in this organization, you make more money than the owner of the company, and you have all the benefits that go along with being just an employee, so you get more money, more flexibility, and less responsibility all because you have amazing sales skills.

If you are eyeing the highest paying job in any organization, it is going to be in the sales department. · at is where the opportunity is. Engineers, doctors, lawyers, professors, and other such people who have a valuable skill set and are highly educated, unfortunately, are pigeonholed into positions where they cannot make a lot of money. For instance, doctors don't make much money unless they specialize in something like heart surgery or brain surgery. And even in order to be able to get those practices off the ground, they have to be great salespeople as well.

· erefore, if you ever want to make any money in this world, you have to know how to sell. I alluded to it in the previous chapter. If you are providing what you believe is a six figure value, but you are not making six figures, that tells me that you are unable to sell your employer on giving you the bonuses and the commissions that you should have in order to make big money in your position or a sales position in your employers company. So, for example if you learn to sell properly then you can sell your way internally to more compensation and better positions within the organization. Now you see why learning to sell is so important? Obviously, how much is that costing you? How many promotions will you be passed up for if you can't sell? Too many so you need to learn to sell!

Whether you own your own business or you are an employee, you have to have master sales skills. ·e more you can master sales, the greater the opportunities you are going to have. Employees who think they don't have to sell are just simply shortsighted, and those employees never make any money. It does not matter if you are an engineer, and you fully plan on staying in the engineering department of your company. ·e ability to go to your bosses and sell them on yourself, and on ideas that you have, some changes you want to make, and strategies you want to implement, are not going to happen if you don't have true sales skills.

What does sales mean? It means the ability to persuade, convince, and—I hate to use the word, but it is an accurate one—manipulate. Now, manipulation can be used for good or for bad. In this case, we always use manipulation for good. I don't manipulate people in any negative or nefarious ways at all; I always manipulate them for their benefit and they are always greater than mine.

So, when I do use high-level skills and techniques to persuade and convince someone, and yes, manipulate them, I am doing so for what I know is their own benefit. ·is goes for all the customers, employees, and employers I have to sell. Remember that you should never use your power of persuasion to trick or deceive anyone. And never sell someone something unless you know it will benefit them at least twice as much as whatever you are asking for. ·at's a simple rule I always follow. Give at least twice the value for what you are asking for in return. It's ethical, moral and just good business so always provide more than you receive!

Now, let's get into some mechanics of some sales techniques. Of course, I cannot give you the full skillset necessary for you to be a great salesperson within this chapter alone, but I want to at least give you the framework for what you do need to know and need to learn so you can begin immediately. You can find a lot more about sales skills in my YouTube videos, my social media platforms as well as my online courses. But for now, let's simply focus on the six key skills needed to start to become great at sales. I call them the "Magnificent Six" and they are, Speaking with Confidence, Working Knowledge, Attention, Value, Persuasion and Closing. · ey are not exclusive of each other and hence work together in concert as pieces of a full orchestra that equal great sales skills.

· e first skill of the Six is that you first have to know how to actually talk well. Whether you are working in telephone sales, internet sales, or face-to-face sales, the ability to communicate your solution effectively is going to be vital in setting up any good sale. Being a good salesperson is not simply having a couple of tricks up your sleeve where you can trap people into bad decisions. · at is a far too often used and shortsighted approach, which is what I call "Strong Arming", and it will never work long term, and certainly will not work on anything that is of a high-ticket value.

True quality sales skills do not come from maneuvering; they come from persuasion. So, in order to actually persuade somebody, you need to be able to make a valid argument with speaking in a way they would believe is trustworthy. If the person listening to your argument does not trust you as a person, they are certainly not going to be persuaded to buy. · erefore, the first thing you have to learn is how to speak well to gain the personal credibility needed to be taken seriously and hence truly listed to by your prospect.

Now, I am not saying that you have to become a great public speaker, and you have to be comfortable speaking in front of five thousand people. But you do need to be able to speak with people professionally and reasonably. You need to use proper language, syntax, and verbiage, as well as the right tone, tempo, pitch, and rhythm. All these things go into being a great communicator and hence a great salesperson. If you are not a good talker, you are not going to be a good communicator or salesperson. It is just that simple.

So, what do you want to do? You want to speak clearly and concisely. Do not repeat yourself. Speak from your chest. Sit up straight. Stand, if you have to, because that does help. Make sure you are moving your hands, and you are really involved in speaking. · is will make sure you have the right tone and tempo, which is a huge deal. Many bad salespeople I see speak in a monotone and very basic pitch level. Nobody wants to listen to a low-energy monotone person speak. You need to have a great pitch and inflection in your tone, and you certainly need to have a lot of energy. Of course, do not flail your arms too wildly but in a way that conveys and amplifies your message naturally.

A simple trick to practice this is to actually record yourself speaking. · ink of the last argument that you had with your spouse, your children, or your parents. Take that argument, and record yourself. Record yourself making the point you were trying to make then. How does your voice sound? How is your tone or your tempo? If you don't master those things, nothing else is going to work. · ese are the basics. · ere are a lot of videos, including many that I have, on social media and YouTube, regarding the right pitch and tone, and ability to speak to make your argument heard. · at is the first requirement in becoming a good salesperson.

· e next key thing you need for great selling is confidence that comes from the Working Knowledge of your solution. No one wants to listen to someone who does not have confidence. You have to be confident about what you are talking about. If you are not confident, you have to ask yourself, "Why am I not confident in this? Am I not confident because I don't have the right knowledge of the product or the service I am selling?" And that is likely the case and if so, go study your good or service until you know that you have a great working knowledge in what you are trying to sell. If you are not at a confident level in what you are trying to sell, at least from an understanding point of view, it will be very tough to communicate the solution it provides to the customer effectively. You certainly don't need engineering skills to sell a wrench, but you do need to know how the utility of how a wrench works and what problems it solves for the customer. Ask how would they use it? When would they use it? Why would it be a huge benefit for them? You have to know these things; otherwise, you would not have any confidence in your argument for them to buy. For good sales skills, a confident working knowledge of the product or service is a must.

You also need to be confident in who you are. When you first pitch to somebody, you have to just look at them and introduce yourself, and do so well. You have to say, "Hi. My name is Cory. How are you doing today?" And, politely, but respectfully, you have to ask for their attention. If you don't get their attention, they are not going to listen to you. Whenever I am giving a pitch, the first thing I have to do is get their attention.

· e two easiest ways to get someone's attention on a base level are going to be by having both a working knowledge of the solution as well as to be confidently assertive. Now, some people like to get attention by wearing flashy clothes, getting out of a fancy car, speaking loudly, or saying something crazy. · ose things will get you attention, but that is the wrong kind of attention to be great at sales. Your prospect is not going to be impressed by your flashy anything let alone if you are arrogant. · ey may be amused, and you may have their attention for five seconds, but they are not going to want to listen to your solutions on anything and certainly will not buy from you.

So how do you get the right attention? First, sound important and be important. Act as if you are a working knowledge expert of your solution. Now, it does not mean you should be condescending. It simply means you should act as if you are convinced that the solution you have is going to be the greatest thing this person has ever heard of for their particular problem. So, whenever I am pitching a solution to someone, I know beforehand that this is going to not only be a solid solution but will also offer at least twice the value for my customer. If it isn't, I need to rediscover why my solution isn't worth twice the value of what it costs, and I better make it worth that or offer a different more valuable solution.

If I know that I'm going to pitch a valuable solution to somebody, you better believe I have no problem getting their attention. I am going to be confident; I am going to walk up to them, and I am going to pitch it strongly and aggressively, and that alone will get their attention. You don't need ridiculous tactics to get attention and the quirky slimy sales techniques we see in the movies are simply silly and do not work. Be firm, give firm handshakes, and introduce yourself appropriately but confidently. · at is how you get the right kind of attention needed to sell well.

· e next skill is how to properly persuade. Now you have to learn how to pitch in a persuasive way. Simply, you have to tell someone why the solution you are giving them is going to be amazing for them. Make it all about them, and never about you. Also, base your persuasion pitch on benefits, not features. I will give a prime example. If I am selling a car, I can tell someone, "Oh, these seats are made of the highest-grade leather there is. · is engine has six hundred horsepower. It goes from zero to sixty in 3.9 seconds. · is car will stop in a hundred feet. · is car turns heads. Sounds okay, right? Wrong! · ese persuasion points are features, not benefits.

Benefits are the things the person will experience as they drive the car. For instance, with the leather seats, "· ese seats are made of one hundred percent Italian leather. · ey are going to cuddle you and comfort you while you drive. After a long drive, you are literally going to feel refreshed." · at is the benefit they will experience of the seats being high grade leather not just the feature. Now, with the benefit being used instead the person believes it is something that is going to benefit them personally, and it can be even life changing thereby adding a high level of value to that solution. I would also talk about the safety features of the vehicle. Talk about saving their and their children's lives. · at is certainly of high value. Also, when you are persuading by using benefits, always understand that the benefits have to be life changing. It cannot be something that is slightly better otherwise it will not have the high value perceived by the buyer for you to effectively close and provide twice the value of the money you are asking!

So, again, with a car sale as an example, I would say, "With six hundred horsepower, this car is going to get you in and out of traffic and tight spots lickety-split. Obviously, if you find yourself in a situation where you need to get out of the way, you have the power to do it." Here, I coupled the fact that the car has six hundred horsepower with the ability for that to move it quickly and be safe. · at is a life-changing benefit. All benefits can be made life changing. You simply need to discover how to do it and get a little creative. By doing so you will increase the value of what you are selling dramatically which will lead to easier closes and a happier customer. And naturally by doing so it almost always creates that "twice the value" aspect to the prospect, which we are committed to provide.

· e next skill and the by far the biggest skill for great sales is learning how to properly close. Saddle up because this skill does get slightly more complex than the other five and hence it is the single biggest weakness of any salesperson that ever lived. But don't worry there are very solid techniques that will ensure you can achieve a very high close ratio. Let's start first with what a trail close is. Now, a trial close is similar to a close, except in the fact that you are not really anticipating a close when using it, although a close can happen using your trial close that is not its first purpose. What you are really looking for first and foremost is raising objections to the close. As a good salesperson, you never want to fear objections. Bad salespeople fear objections and really fear the word "no." However, until you get the objections and the "no" out of the way, you cannot create a "yes" and a close in its place.

Therefore, if you want to learn to close you have to get the objections revealed as quickly, clearly and as directly as possible. You don't want them to stay hidden. Anybody with a hidden objection will not close. Hence, you need the objections to be conveyed to you by the buyer quickly and clearly, and that is where trial closing comes in. Trial closing is a very simple technique but often overlooked or misunderstood. To do it properly you simply ask for the order. Now, a lot of bad salespeople, unfortunately, will not ask for the order and instead get stuck selling features hoping the buyer just closes themselves by asking "Can I buy this?". Good luck on waiting for prospects to simply ask you if it's ok for them to buy. So how exactly do you transition to a trail close? A simple example would be. "Mary, I have told you about all the high value benefits you'll receive by buying this vehicle. I have told you about the life-changing things this can do for you and you agreed with me on all of them. Therefore, Mary there's nothing left to do but just make this car yours so let's sign the paperwork right now and complete the sale."

Now, there are only two things that could happen after that trial close: Either the buyer is going to say, "Sounds good. Let us do it," and now it turns into a real, full close; or, the prospect is going to tell you why they are not ready to close and offer an objection by which it worked perfectly as a trial close. This is going to give me the ability to overcome the objection they present, overcome it with either another benefit or calm their concerns and then trial close again. This can go on several times for several objections but if I handle them right each time I will eventually move to close after one of the trial closes. The only difference between a trail close and a full close is when the buyer agrees to the purchase.

Remember all objections can be overcome if your solution is genuine. Now, if you are selling something that is not real or does not do what you are promising, then you obviously cannot overcome all objections because the one objection you can't overcome is the one where the customer knows the value is not in your solution. If that is the case then revaluate right there and determine if your solution is really going to solve the problem or not and if it has twice the value as the price. If it's not both then you are selling something unethically, and that is not right. Stop doing it right now. Anything you ever sell should be worth twice as much to the buyer in the form of the solutions and benefits it provides as it costs. If you don't thoroughly believe that you are going to give the buyer twice the real value in anything you sell them than the money it is going to cost them, don't do it.

How is "twice as valuable" determined? Simply because of the benefits the solution provides. Why are the benefits twice as valuable? Because you made them life changing. So, if you truly have life-changing benefits as part of your persuasion pitch on your good or service, then you absolutely have the full confidence that it is worth at least twice as much money as you're asking. If so then there can never be any real objections simply stalls and or excuses due to the buyer being unconfident in themselves or a part of your communication was not clear. · is is actually very common even if the benefits were clear and the value was properly persuaded. Still there can be stalls and delays simply based upon the buyer not having self confidence in their decision making. When this occurs do not panic. Simply at this point before you circle back to persuade them with more or restated benefits you want to take the solution away from them in the form of a "takeaway". I call this level of sales "Inception Selling" and it works amazingly. With practice and learning a properly excocted takeaway can be very simple to perform. You simply state to the buyer. "Mary if this car isn't a good fit for you, I absolutely do not want you to buy it. In fact, I think until we solve all of your concerns you shouldn't even consider buying this car." If it was simply an excuse or confusion on the buyer's part then by simply doing a takeaway you will actually increase their desire to buy it.

Oftentimes the purpose of a stall tactic or an excuse from a buyer is that they simply don't trust you. · ey may not have the confidence in their decision because they are unsure you have been honest about the solution being more valuable than the cost. Using my "Inception Selling System" in this situation is natural and the easiest and most effective way to overcome these final excuses. You can create the close by simply telling them that maybe this solution just isn't for them and you really don't want them to do something they are not completely comfortable with. By doing so they will instantly desire it more and their confidence will be re-instilled that your persuasion pitch of the solution was honest and trustworthy and therefore they will be more than willing to move to close. If not then they may still have a hidden objection and perhaps you did not do as good of a job as you thought in your persuasion pitch of selling benefits and not features. If that's the case then move back to probing for the hidden objection.

So how do you identify and overcome hidden objections that prevent the close? Well, the vast majority of hidden objections are not objections at all; they are just excuses, and you have to be aware of the difference between the two. Somebody who says, "Oh, my spouse is not here, and I cannot make the decision alone," that is really an excuse, not a true objection. Let us face it; they talked about it before they came to you. · ey have probably talked about this a million times. Whether they say it is their boss or their spouse, it is the same objection. Be aware that they have discussed these solutions and these problems before, and they have said to themselves that if a solution ever presented itself that made a lot of sense, and had great, life-changing benefits, that they would go ahead and buy.

Now, what do you do with excuses? Acknowledge them, but respond with, "Look, if you were not convinced that you wanted a solution, we would never even be talking. You know the benefits you will receive are going to outweigh any of the costs of the money. Let's just go ahead and get this deal done." If you have sold the benefits properly in your persuasion pitch of benefits, and the benefits are life changing, the sale will happen naturally all without strong arming.

Now, how to overcome a true objection? · e first rule in overcoming objections is to isolate the objection. Sometimes, objections are not quite as clear as they should be. Never be afraid to ask again if you don't fully understand the objection of your prospect. You can do no wrong in asking questions. If the objection my buyer has is unclear to me, I simply would say, "Mary, I do not quite understand exactly what your hesitation is. Can you explain it to me in a little more detail?" Usually, this will prod them into giving you more details and insight into their way of thinking.

· en you have to ask yourself, why is the buyer's objection greater than the benefits in their eyes? You see any objection that becomes the core reason not to buy is simply due to the fact that the buyer does not believe that the benefits have twice the value of the cost. If I my benefits persuasion pitches are made on life-changing events, then how can their objections be greater than my life-changing benefits? · ey cannot. So, again, if you have not given life-changing benefits, you are going to run into more objections when you trail close. If you get stuck on an objection never argue or resort to arm twisting with the buyer. Always simply do a takeaway that I teach in my "Inception Selling System" and then go back and redo your benefits and persuasion pitch properly. If I have truly given life-changing benefits, I hardly run into objections as the buyer clearly perceives the value of my solution and by doing the takeaway at key points along the way they in fact truly desire my solution. Sometimes buyers simply need reassurance that the solution will work for them and that is where your confidence and working knowledge expertise comes in. If that is their final excuse, I simply state the benefits again and make it clear on how they will solve the problem they indicated they wanted solved and then provide life changing and high value benefits. As I do those two things well, their last concerns are typically just little excuses that are easily overcome. · en, I move to close again and close.

As a final point in this limited training, how does proper closing work? Just like the five-year-old would show you in a department store with their parent, the closing has to be direct, firm, and absolute. It cannot be convoluted or wishy-washy. You simply have to say, "Let's do this". "Let's get it done". "Let's get it signed." "Let's write it up." Simply ask. Once all the objections are dealt with, and they have truly realized the benefits far outweigh the costs, they will close every single time and be happy to do so. Learning my "Inception Selling System" will require a lot of practice but once you master these skills you will be unstoppable in your sales abilities; I promise you that.

CHAPTER 16

Pufling It All Together: The Big Picture

At this point in the book, you obviously have seen all that goes into maximizing your now, and also maximizing your future. And as I have made the point over and over again it starts with work ethic. ·ere simply is no getting around it. You have to put in the work, and you have to be willing to make the sacrifices. If you are employed, the sacrifice has to be fifty to fifty-five hours a week at work and sever hours of learning. Anything less than that means you are leaving a lot of your potential untapped. You have to be willing to put in the work and the time, not only to get the job done but also to increase your skill set, to prove to your employer that you are serious and dedicated and that you are willing to do what it takes to get the job done and be a valuable part of the team. If you are a business owner, it has to be the Blackjack 7-7-7 rule: seven days a week, 7:00 a.m. to 7:00 p.m., because anything less is probably going to cause you to fail.

By putting in the work first, everything else can fall into place. Without it, nothing else has a chance. You have to put in the time to reap the rewards. Let's again compare it to the gym. If you are not going to the gym and putting in the time and the effort, and following the correct diet, then what chance do you have to get six pack abs? None, it is not going to happen.

· e next thing that goes into making good money, besides the work, is the skill set. As we have discussed, the skill set only develops when you are making the sacrifice to put in the work. Unless you are actually putting in the work and sacrifice to do it consistently, you are not going to get good at what you are doing. If you are not putting in the time at the gym, lifting heavy weights, and sweating and pushing yourself every day, will you ever get good at lifting weights? No. You will never achieve proper form, technique, and ability to train your body.

· e same rules apply regarding pushing your skills, your mind, and your will. If you are not willing to go to work for fifty-five hours a week, then how is your mind ever going to get pushed to get better? If your mind does get better, but your will to achieve and succeed does not improve, how will you ever be able to become good at anything? I believe the mind is just like a muscle. · e more it is trained, the harder it is worked, the stronger it gets. If you want your mind and your abilities to be their strongest, you have to put them under tension. You have got to challenge yourself, just like being in the gym. If you don't challenge it, it will not grow, and you will not improve as a critical thinker and a better problem solver. · ese things are vital to being successful in this world, and you have to earn them by working them to their potential.

Beyond just putting in the time and the work in order to achieve a good skill set, you also need to study. You have to go out there and get the knowledge you require. You have to read this book over and over again. You have to read other books, watch training videos, take training classes, attend seminars and get a great coach to push you. Do everything you can get to develop the skill set you need, especially when it comes to speaking and sales. You need to have great speaking skills because you need to have great sales skills. If you don't have those two skills, then the other skills will not be utilized to their potential, and you will not be able to maximize your current and future opportunities. So, keep learning. You will hear me say it here and everywhere else, "Learn to earn. If you don't learn, you will never earn."

So, let's say you follow the lessons I have laid out in this book, what will you have? You will have a great work ethic, you will be working fifty to fifty-five hours a week, and because of that your skills will improve rapidly. Next you will achieve a rapid pay increase. It does not matter if you are a janitor, an attendant working in the McDonald's drive-through window, or an Attorney. If you are working harder, getting better, and your skills are improving, so will your pay. Now, what do you do with the pay increases? You make sure you get your credit score higher, because the ability to leverage cheaper money is going to be a key for you to increase income long term and to live a better lifestyle for the same expense.

You will be able to buy nicer cars and houses at a lower interest rate. You will be able to get credit cards and use them for what they are good for, which is getting points and building a credit score. You can use the points to get free travel and cash back. · ese things all add up over time and can make a huge difference in your income. · e money you save from having good credit as well as the benefits you can get from the rewards of having premium credit cards together are huge when it comes to maximizing your disposable income.

Of course, you have to make sure the bad debt is gone. If you have any old, bad debts, they need to be settled up right away. · e faster you can settle them up, the better off you are going to be, and the faster you will get that credit score rising. Even a debt that is not necessarily bad from the perspective of being a write-off or negative on your credit can be refinanced if the leverage is too expensive. For example, if you have a car loan at 15–16 percent; if you get your credit up you can flip your high interest rates to lower interest rates. · is, again, will make another huge increase in the amount of your disposable income.

By using all of the strategies I have laid out in this book you will be able to increase your disposable income and begin using the 50/5 rule. Now, imagine a life with 50 percent more disposable income, not several years from now but within a few months. After all, the name of this book is Maximize Your Now, and all the tips, tricks, strategies, and secrets that I have mentioned in this book are all designed to increase your disposable income right here, right now, and maximize your now so you can create a more prosperous future.

Now that you have the financial basics down, remember the other chapters of the book. Remember to move through your world with a positive mentality. No, Mondays don't suck; Mondays are awesome. "I can't wait for Monday morning." · at is what you have to tell yourself. "I can't wait to bust my butt all week. I can't wait to get better this week. I can't wait to work longer and harder this week. I love my job, and I like my demanding boss." · ese are the things you have to tell yourself, and you have got to show up every single day with a positive mentality. A positive mentality is going to lead to great things.

If anything does not go your way, lament for thirty seconds. However, on the thirty-first second, you better be moving on to the solution. You are not going to sit there and dwell on the problems. You are going to quickly transition into the solutions. As a matter of fact, there is no such thing as a problem. · ere is only a lack of a solution. Start seeking the solutions right now.

After learning these new techniques, you can now start moving with purpose. You have a reason to be happy, you have your **why**. Your why is to help people. Your happiness is derived from helping people, whether it is your family, your boss, your customers, your coworkers, or any of their families. All your thoughts and actions are designed to help other people and bring them benefits and success. If you are consistently bringing people around you benefits, and if everything you are doing is for the benefit of others, you are going to wake up every morning happy and eager to contribute. You will always feel wanted and desired. · at is the key to happiness, not fancy stuff, not a new car, not a new house or a fancy vacation. · e key to happiness is, and always will be, how much you help others.

Now, it would not be a good summary if we did not discuss the number one skill that we need. We need to be able to sell. If you cannot sell, you will not be able to convey your ideas to people, and you will not be able to persuade people. Again, your purpose is to benefit people by offering them life-changing solutions. Now, if you cannot sell, how is the world going to know of these life-changing benefits? How are you going to get those life-changing benefits to your customers, clients, boss, coworkers, and employees? How are you going to affect the world in a positive way if you cannot convince anybody of your solutions? You cannot. · at is why you have to learn how to sell.

Now, these things are the basics to leading a successful, happy, prosperous life. With this, you are going to help people and bring life-changing benefits to the world. · at is the new you. · at is now you—the untapped potential—that was always there. · is is how you're going to MAXIMIZE YOUR NOW. · is is the essence of why we are here. · e purpose of your life is to help others, and there is absolutely nothing wrong with becoming very prosperous while you do it. You can make a lot of money by helping a lot of people. · e more people you help, and the bigger problems you solve for them, the more money you are going to make. Never lose sight of that.

Now, the money you make is not just for fancy cars, fancy houses, and fancy vacations. It is also to take that money and put it into the world and help everyone you can. It means you can help people, provide more, and essentially give more and more of yourself. · e more money you make, the more of you there is to go around to more people. If you are genuinely helping people and changing their lives for the better, there is no reason to be ashamed of making great money. Be out there, and get doing both.

Scale it all. Scale every aspect and every chapter of this book. Everything we have talked about in this book—you can scale every part of it. You can scale your work ethic, your skill set, even your ability to help more people with bigger problems. Do it, and do it now. Instantly, you will feel yourself change and grow, and you will feel better, happier, and more productive. You will change lives.

When can it start? Right now.

When are you going to do it? Right now. We got this!

CPSIA information can be obtained
at www.ICGtesting.com
Printed in the USA
BVHW012144280521
608097BV00008B/710